OH
SH*T
I'm in Sales?

An Entrepreneur's Guide to

Making Sales Her New BFF

SUSAN TRUMPLER

Unstoppable Women in Business

Published by

Hybrid Global Publishing

301 E 57th Street

4th Floor

New York, NY 10022

Copyright © 2022 by Susan Trumpler

Manufactured in the United States of America.

Trumpler, Susan

*Oh Sh*t, I'm in Sales? An Entrepreneur's Guide to Making Sales Your BFF*

     ISBN: 978-1-951943-93-6

eBook: 978-1-951943-94-3

LCCN: 2021920221

Cover design by: Natasha Clawson

Copyediting by: Wendie Pecharsky

Interior design by: Suba Murugan

Author photo by: Tricia Turpenoff Photography

www.unstoppablewomeninbusiness.com

TABLE OF CONTENTS

Most women whom I work with definitely did not go into business so they could become professional salespeople. None of them woke up one day and said to themselves, "My life would be complete if I could only have the chance to convince someone that they really need to buy something from me. And wouldn't it be great to spend most of my days thinking of ways that I could get strangers to want to solve a problem they didn't really know they had? Yup! That would be awesome!" If you are someone who had this dream, I haven't met you yet. And to be completely transparent, you can stop reading this book, you most likely don't need it!

Becoming really good at sales is more often than not an afterthought for women who are super excited about starting their own business.

Now, everyone has their own reasons when it comes to why they are self-employed, but most involve the fact that they are *really* good at something and want to help others get good at it too. There is something they are passionate about, something they have figured out over the years and have some sense of pride knowing they have "expertise" in this area. Then one day, this little seed of a thought forms in their mind about how cool it would be to spend all their time doing this thing for a living. They dream of making money doing it, that's for sure. But rarely does the thought of HOW they will make that money enter into their minds. If it does, they have watched or listened to some online guru tell them that all they have to do is put it out there and "they will buy." Kind of like Kevin Costner in *Field of Dreams:* Build it and they will come.

Let's take life coaches as an example. Your traditional life coach has most likely done a lot of self-development work. At one point in their life, they found themselves deeply unhappy about some aspect of their life. Maybe it was over a relationship, maybe it was over money. Sometime in their life they felt that something was lacking and they were not quite fulfilled. So they went on a journey to successfully improve their life. They most likely hired a coach who was amazing and helped them through a process that yielded great results. The transformation wasn't easy, but the exhilaration of having their life transformed created a renewed sense of purpose for them. Every day as they walk through life experiencing a completely new way of living, they say to themself, "I can't believe how great I feel and I have GOT to help other people feel the same way!"

Another example might be a woman in a dull job, working for a company where she enjoys what she does. She's very good at it, but she feels somewhat unfulfilled. Day in and day out, she goes to work to make someone else money. Maybe she isn't respected the way she would like to be. Maybe she just doesn't respect the people around her or the values of the company she works for. But there is something nagging at her deep inside that causes her to think, "Hey, I could be doing this for myself, in my own business, instead of putting money into the pockets of other people. I'm going to start my own business."

There are a million scenarios about why women want to build their own empire, but none of them started because that voice inside of her was saying, "I can't wait to go out there and sell myself!"

Can I get an amen here, lady??

That brings us to how the idea for *OH SH!T I'm in Sales?* was born. As a sales coach and business strategist, I have witnessed many of these moments of awakening for my clients and for women that I meet when networking, that painful moment when an entrepreneur realizes that to achieve the goal of becoming a successful business owner, they have to become a successful salesperson. Yup, this is the "OH SH!T" moment that hits them squarely between the eyes and the fear and dread start to bubble up in their gut. They realize they have gotten themselves into a pickle. To be successful at their dream, they have to learn to love the one thing they never thought they would ever have to do—SELL!!!

This is the make-or-break moment for most entrepreneurs. If they could visualize a road that forks not once, but three times, leaving three different paths they could choose to go down, that's where they are, right at that junction in the road of sales. If they choose the first path, they stay in fear, dread, and avoidance of sales and eventually their business will wither and die. The second path is where they dig in their heels in and work like heck to figure out how to DO sales. While this path is leading them closer to running a successful business, it's still a tough road to follow. While they're going through the motions, doing all the things they *need* to do to generate revenue, they're still in resistance and it's an uphill climb that can be tiring and only yield sporadic results. But the third path is the choice that leads them toward embracing the fact that sales can be fun and that they don't have to resist or avoid it. They can make sales their BFF and watch their business soar!

I consider it my job in this book to help you understand exactly how easy it is to choose that third path and never look back again. Whether you would classify your current relationship with sales as toxic or just "passing friends," this book will help you understand why you want sales to be your new BFF and how you can get there.

We're going to take a journey together that will be interesting and hopefully fun for you. First, we are going to dive into what I really mean when I say you have to make sales your new BFF. Whenever there is a problem to solve, and, believe me, if you don't enjoy selling, you do have a problem, gaining an awareness and deep understanding of what the problem is and where it comes from is the first step to solving it.

After that, I'm going to introduce HOW to not only enjoy selling, but will do it by teaching you a repeatable process that will help you create a completely new perspective around sales. My desire for you is to use this process for the rest of your life. We will call it your "automatic attitude adjustment tool." You will have it in your back pocket and think of me each time you find yourself in a situation where you have fallen back into old ways of thinking about sales. You will pull it out, work through the steps, and get back on track in a heartbeat.

Along the way, I will share stories of other women who are recovering sales haters. We will talk about where they started, what they did to shift their perspective of sales, and the results they got once they successfully followed that third path. What I've learned from my over 15 years of being involved in sales training is this: People learn best from each other. I can transfer information to you (that's another way of saying teach), but the learning actually happens when it is set into context that makes sense to you. Something you can really resonate with. So I've got lots of those examples for you in this book as well.

Learning to get comfortable with selling can actually be fun. Trust me, I got you on this one! Let's get started!

CHAPTER 1

MAKING SALES YOUR BFF

One night, a casual acquaintance of mine, someone who I knew from a women's group I was a member of, called and asked if I was interested in coming to a wine tasting in her home that upcoming Friday night. Because I had no life at the time, I hesitated for about a tenth of a second and said, "Sure!! What time?" I'm not someone you would think of as a wallflower so it didn't bother me to think about the fact that I wouldn't really know anyone there. I can generally talk to anyone and especially if it was about one of my favorite subjects—wine!

Little did I know that this was the beginning of an amazing relationship with a group of eight women that has lasted for more than 20 years. As we mixed and mingled with each other that first night and were treated to a guided wine tasting experience that the hostess put together, it was almost like seeing the individual stars in the sky start swirling into a pattern and becoming the cosmos. By the end of the night, we all decided that we had so much fun, that we wanted to do it again. We decided to meet monthly and rotate the hosting responsibilities. This meant that each month someone would organize the wine tasting: naming the varietal that everyone would bring to sample, then act as "master of ceremonies" as each person presented their bottle. Of course, there was food involved. Lots of food and, man, can these Southern women cook!!

We called ourselves the "Winey Women" and decided to meet on the first Friday of every month—no excuses—to learn more about wine and each other. We took this commitment to each other seriously. If someone said they couldn't make it to one of our gatherings because of another commitment, we would say collectively, "What part of 'First Friday' do you not understand?"

In the beginning, we were very serious about following wine tasting protocols, changing glasses between the reds and whites, reading the wine notes, and scoring the wines on the bouquet, legs, and mouth feel of each wine we tasted. But it didn't take too long before we were enjoying each other's company as much as, or more than, the actual wine itself.

We went deep in our conversations, getting to know one another at a soul-enriching level. As the years went by, we got to know what made each one of us tick. We laughed and cried together and would do anything to help one another out. We even started to meet outside of our First Friday gatherings. We traveled places, went on vacations to Napa and other destinations, and generally had a ball in what we called "doing life" together. The best part is that because we got to know one another at such a deep level, we felt safe and had a craving to spend more time in one another's company. Because... that's what BFF's do, right?

RELATIONSHIP BUILDING 101

So by this point in my story you may be saying, "Ummmm, Susan... what does your Winey Women group have to do with this book?"

Oh, girl! There is a connection!

It's all about what it takes to build a relationship. Follow me here for just one minute and it will all begin to be very clear to you. When it comes down to it, relationships are formed in your mind. Here is an example of how that works. Have you ever met someone and taken an immediate dislike to them? You know what I mean, your initial thought. I call this your "Spidey-sense." It might have been that they just weren't your cup of tea. Then, after spending a little time together, you find that they are different from you first imagined and you slowly begin to change your opinion, and before you know it, you find that you really enjoy hanging out with them.

Am I the only one?? I think not! This happens to people all the time. But the question is, what changed? The person hasn't changed. You haven't changed. What has changed is all in your head! Your thoughts about them have changed. As you start thinking about who you think they are, quite often you start feeling more connected and open to becoming friends. Again, I have to reiterate, nothing really changes except your thoughts about them. Hence, evidence for my statement that relationships reside in your brain.

And that brings us to your relationship with sales. When I say it that way, you almost imagine a tall, dark, handsome man standing in front of you named "Sales."

But no! Your relationship with sales is an INTERNAL relationship!! It's a relationship that resides within the part of you that has sales responsibilities. It's your thoughts about WHO YOU ARE in relationship to selling. It's the most intimate relationship you can have because it is *within* yourself. But it can be a relationship filled with animosity and loathing. It's really BIZARRE!

IT ALWAYS STARTS WITH YOU

There are so many facets of you as a person. You might be a mom, you are definitely a businessperson, you may be someone's friend or maybe their partner, you can be a daughter, and maybe even someone's sister. You play so many roles in your life. And the interesting thing is that you have very specific thoughts about yourself in each and every one of those roles.

The part of you that is responsible for generating revenue, in other words selling, is just one of the many facets of you.

So here is the bottom line. When you are at war with selling for your business, you are at war with yourself! And, woman, that does not feel good at all! Not only does it feel horrible rejecting an essential part of you that has important responsibilities, but the ramifications are also debilitating to your business.

Small businesses are notorious for falling like dominos within the first five years of opening their proverbial doors. Why? Lack of sufficient cash flow. The money coming in doesn't cover the overhead and salary needed to keep the business going. We've all seen this scenario play out. Someone tells us about their new business idea. They are flush with excitement and enthusiasm, getting everything set up: the website, the branding, their programs or products. So much fun! But within a couple of years, they are worn out and beaten down and the next thing you hear, they've gone back into corporate to get a j.o.b. There can be a lot of reasons that a business goes under. But more often than not, if it is because of a cash-flow issue, the underlying culprit usually is that Mama didn't learn how to make friends with sales. Most likely, she ignored the most important activities in her business—sales—swept them under the rug, put them at the bottom of her to-do list day after day. Oh, she thinks she "tried." She bought lots of courses, maybe she even worked with a coach to help her learn HOW TO SELL, but at the end of the day, she just wasn't comfortable selling. She stayed on that proverbial first path on the sales road... the one that kept her in a place where she stayed in fear, dread, and avoidance of sales.

When I sense that a client is deeply dug into this path, I worry for them. I have to work with them to understand that they have no choice but to make a U-turn, and get back to that fork in the road, choose the path that takes them toward making friends with sales. And I help them get there using the tools you will read about in this book. I am always so grateful that they were courageous enough to do the work in time to save their business and themselves from a lot of heartache.

The way I think about it is this: Most women business owners' relationship with sales is more like a "frenemy" than a BFF. Remember my story about how I became BFFs with all of my Winey Women? We spent time together, did things we enjoyed, took time to get to know each other well, stood up for each other because we cared and respected each other.

That, my friend, is the key to making sales your BFF. The first thing you will want to do is perform a complete attitude adjustment on the way you look at the part of you that sells. No more saying you feel sleazy or pushy. Stop thinking of yourself as selfish and money-grubbing. STOP IT!

Oh my gosh! I just cracked myself up. Every time I hear or think of the phrase "STOP IT" -- and it is always in capital letters in my mind because I am shouting it -- I think of the *Bob Newhart Show*. Bob in real life was a comedian, but on his show he played a therapist and had a great sense of humor, very dry and witty. Okay, I know, a lot of you are too young to remember this show. It was on television in the '80s, which I know is before many of you were born. But do yourself a favor, go to YouTube and type STOP IT and Bob Newhart into the search bar. You will see a clip of exactly what I'm talking about. It's hysterical!

For those of you who don't want to take the time to do that, I will give you a quick synopsis of the scene that I'm talking about. Bob has a client in his office and she tells him she is afraid of the thoughts she has about being buried alive. As a therapist will do, Bob listens, asks her questions, and gets a good sense for the angst this woman is feeling because of her fear of small spaces. Then Bob says the solution is simple. He has two words for her and they are STOP IT! Just STOP IT! If you watch the clip, you will be laughing just as the fake audience was laughing. His timing and delivery are perfect, but that's not the real reason you laugh. The real laughter comes from the fact that his advice is ludacris as if it was just that easy to change the way you are thinking about something by saying to yourself, "JUST STOP IT!" a majority of our problems would be solved.

Okay, let me land this plane by telling you a story about a client of mine. The story is true, but the name has been changed to protect the innocent!

RELATIONSHIP REALITY CHECK

Kathy was a member of the Success Collaborative, a group coaching program that I run that also includes one-on-one time with me. It was a Friday afternoon and we were having an urgent, spot-coaching session that she had popped into my calendar.

I got on the call with her and asked, "Hey! Kath, what's up? How can I support you?"

Kathy went into a diatribe about a prospect who was not returning her call. She was certain that the reason was that the prospect thought she was pushy and too expensive. Kathy continued to project verbal vomit at me for another minute or two after which I told her to take a breath, slow down, and tell me the backstory.

Once she settled down a little bit, shook off the emotional weighted blanket she had thrown over her shoulders, and started to relate the facts of the situation, it became very clear to me what was happening. Kathy had conducted a sales consult with a prospect earlier in the week. She got super excited because throughout the call she could tell that this person was her IDEAL client and she could really help them. At the end of the call, she made her offer and the prospective client said she needed to think about it a couple of days and would call Kathy back before the end of the week. Kathy said fine and hung up, feeling a little frustrated but very optimistic.

Ugh! I think. *Have I not taught you anything, girl?*

Fast-forward to Friday afternoon: No call from the potential client. Shocker! Kathy doesn't know what to do next. She doesn't want to call to "bug her." She has all of these thoughts running through her mind about how she is a fraud, and who does she think she is anyway? She's too expensive, the person thought she was being pushy and just wanted to grab her money. She literally said, "I HATE SALES. Why can't I just find someone to sell for me and I will just do what I do best—coach?"

Whoa, Nellie! What? How did she go from thoughts like "the consult went well" to those thoughts about being a failure at sales? How did that happen?

Now the simple thing would have been to tell Kathy to… come on, let's say it together… STOP IT! JUST STOP IT! But, unfortunately, like with Bob's patient, it's never that easy. She may have agreed that she was overreacting and given it a good college try to stop thinking the way she was. But it would pass quickly and she would head back down that same path in no time at all.

Until Kathy truly embraced and showed up in every step of the sales process as someone who is confident and actually *liked* what she was doing, she was going to continue to experience those stress-inducing, wine-guzzling, Oreo-snarfing moments of feeling like a fraud and a failure. And, frankly, that was not going to happen. Not on my watch!

DON'T MAKE IT HARDER THAN IT HAS TO BE...

Making sales your BFF is not hard, but it is a process and it requires some work. Just like my journey with the Winey Women. You may start out as strangers, but over time as you learn how to spend time together having some fun, get to know each other at a deeper level, and find a rhythm of how the relationship will work, you will find that selling can become easy and enjoyable.

But not to be accused of getting all rose-colored-glasses Pollyanna on you, let me just stay real. As in any friendship, there will always be times when things get rocky. You may not feel like spending time together, you may have little squabbles. But, what the heck! Does ANY friendship go smoothly all of the time? Heck no! But what we know more than anything else is that any friend worth having as your BFF is worth fighting for. Great relationships don't just happen; they are cultivated and nurtured with compassion and caring.

That's what the salesperson inside you needs: a BFF who is willing to be by their side no matter what. You want to become each other's "ride or die."

So, let's figure out where this whole frenemy thing with sales comes from in the first place. Everyone knows the first step to solving any issue is to admit there's a problem and that is part of the discovery work you do to figure out where the problem came from.

I will meet you in the next chapter!

CHAPTER 2

MAKING SALES YOUR BFF

My daughter was reading a self-development book the other day and she looked up at me and said, "Did you know that every cell in your body is replaced in seven-year cycles? Supposedly, you become a completely different person at a cellular level every seven years!"

That statement stopped me in my tracks as I took in what she was saying and all the implications behind it. To think that every day, our bodies are evolving and literally forming a new vessel without any conscious effort on our part just blows my mind. This means that while we go about our day-to-day business, inside you are becoming something brand new. That's pretty freaking awesome, don't you think?

When you really think about what is happening in your body RIGHT NOW as you are reading this book, doesn't it give you a sense of amazement and maybe even a sense of responsibility to care for yourself better? I mean, think about it. You have the option to fuel the vessel that is your body and strengthen it, so the little cell-building army within has everything it needs to help you morph into a new and different person, physically, over time.

But even if we don't provide top-notch fuel, the machine that is your body is going to do its work with whatever you put into it. The results might look a little different (hence my bubble butt that grows whenever I indulge my carb cravings). But nothing stops the little army at work in your body from forming new cells and sloughing off the old ones. It just happens.

THE FORMING OF GRAY MATTER

I'd like you to consider that there is another part of you that forms and creates itself over time without any "conscious" effort on your part, and the quality of its renewal depends on the quality of fuel that you provide it. I'm talking about your mind. Your belief systems are built on thoughts you have over time that create deep grooves in your brain and become thought patterns, which eventually becomes your default thinking.

Researchers claim that the average person has in excess of 6,000 thoughts per day. I don't know about you, but I feel like a superstar in this category, and with most of these thoughts occurring between 3 and 5 in the morning, I'm thinking that my thoughts number well into the tens of thousands.

Scientists call all of those thoughts rambling through your mind "thought worms." Now isn't that attractive? But seriously, here is how the pattern emerges: A thought pops into your mind, seemingly from nowhere, and that starts a chain of thoughts (hence the thought worm). Before you know it, you are 10 thoughts down the line and you can't even remember what started this whole mental rant in the first place. You've been there, right?

You can see this thought worm process played out in Technicolor in a scenario that goes something like this: You are sitting at your computer and thinking of something you need to order from Amazon. So you open a Google browser, go to the Amazon site, type in your user ID and password, and hit enter. As you are waiting for the site to fully load, you might have a thought about your bank balance in the account you will be using to pay for your purchase, so you hit the magic + sign to open another window and dive into your online banking site. You get that page fully loaded and all of a sudden you notice that there has been a charge from a merchant you don't recognize, so you take note of the business name and hit the + sign again. It takes a couple of minutes, but as you do a search on that business and what they do, you are reminded of what you bought... let's just say it was a cool, little app that someone told you about that helps you be more productive. (How ironic, right?) But, after you bought it, you got distracted before you were able to download and install it on your computer. So, yup, you hit the magic + sign again, go to that site, and start the download process because you definitely know you want to be more productive because you can't seem to get the things done that are on your to-do list.

At this point, 15 minutes have passed, there are four browser windows open, and if you are anything like me, you can't even remember what you wanted to buy on Amazon in the first place. PLEASE tell me I'm not alone in this online dance that happens on a daily basis. The sites change, but the thoughts going through my mind unrestricted create browser proliferation, and by the end of the day, I have 20 tabs open and tasks left half completed.

While this becomes a productivity issue, which is not what this book is about, it is a great example of thought worms and how they can drive your physical activity. But I believe the thought worms that manifest in you taking an immediate action are easier to tame because, as in this situation, you have evidence in front of your eyes: a browser full of tabs open that documents the flow of your thoughts and the distraction that can come from those particular thought worms.

What I really want to focus on in this chapter are the thought worms that have taken up residence in your mind for years and years, the ones that form your perspective of how you see the world and what it means to you. Then we can dig into how this applies to your thoughts about selling, so we can tie this all together in something I like to call your "Sales Blueprint," the very essence of how you view your relationship with and how you think about sales today.

THE CLASSIC SALES EXPERIENCE

Let's take a tour of our minds by getting on the tour bus in a situation most of us have been in… buying a car!

My first independent car-buying experience happened, ironically enough, when I was married and wanted to get a car that I knew my husband would not be onboard with. I've always been one of those "get what you want at any cost, but without conflict" kind of people. I knew that asking for forgiveness rather than permission was the way to get the things I wanted during our marriage… hence the reason I am not married now. And that's another topic for another day!

I had gotten a bee in my bonnet that what I needed more than anything was a convertible. My husband didn't think it was a good idea toting two kids under five around in a convertible, something about it not being "practical." Hmmm, if I'd wanted to drive something practical, I would have gotten a minivan, and THAT wasn't going to happen.

So I decided to go off to the dealership on my own and look at the convertible that had been zooming through my dreams for weeks. And may I just say that I WAS being practical because it had a back seat—come on!

So there I was, sitting in the office of a junior salesperson at a luxury car dealership, telling him that I was THINKING about getting a convertible. Something like the bright, shiny, sexy one sitting right behind me on the sales floor.

Now, if this was a Disney movie, he would have sat back in his chair and given me a toothy grin, showing that one of his front teeth was silver and gave off little glimmers when the light hit it. There would have even been a pinging chime as the light hit the tooth, causing sparks to fly.

You know what happened next, right? He said something to the effect of, "Well, little missy, why don't we just go take one of those beauties for a spin? What's your favorite color?"

We proceeded to go on a test drive together, with me driving and him in the passenger seat. I may have made him poop his pants a couple of times because I have what my daddy told me was a "lead foot." He still did a good job making small talk and telling me about all of the amazing features of the car while keeping one eye peeled for oncoming traffic. But the real selling tactics started when we got back to the showroom. I believe you all have been in this situation once or twice in your life. Once he was settled in his desk chair, Mr. Slick started by asking me what kind of monthly payment I was thinking about. (By the way, just in case you don't know, don't EVER answer that question in a car-buying situation. The answer will most likely put them in a position of power that you will never recover from.) I didn't know that at the time, so Miss Trusting (me) told him what I thought to be a comfortable payment.

What happened next was that he had to go to the back, to his manager's office, and "see what they could do." For some reason, the manager could not come out front. The salesperson had to keep going back and forth and back and forth. While he was gone, I had so many thoughts spinning through my mind. I was imagining what it would feel like to be riding with the top down, the sun shining, music blaring—going fast! I started to justify why I deserved a sweet, little ride like her. (Yes, I was already personifying the car, picking out a name.) I started to think about how my husband spent money on things that he wanted for himself all the time. Amazingly enough, the time the salesperson spent with his manager gave me plenty of time to sell myself on how much I wanted that car.

As he went back and forth, he said things like, "I'm really trying hard for you," and "We've never given away such a great car for so little." Finally, he laid down the gauntlet and said something like, "I think I've gotten the manager to come around to our way of seeing things, but he will only do this if you say yes today, before you leave."

At that point, I was putty in his/their hands. They had manipulated me and I sort of knew it, but I didn't care. I wanted that damn car!

Ewwwwww. Even retelling this story makes me feel "sold." Yet at that moment, I couldn't walk away. It was like I was in a trance. I literally went into the dealership to simply get information and perhaps test drive a car I was thinking I might like to buy, and now here I was getting ready to commit based on tactics designed to manipulate and control my actions.

FORMING YOUR SALES BLUEPRINT

Experiences like that, my friend, are some of the building blocks that ultimately create your sales blueprint, in essence, your perspective on selling and the people who are doing it. And it's not just car-buying experiences. There are myriad situations where you may express a mild curiosity about something and a trained salesperson swoops in and you feel like a deer in headlights. You don't want to leave, but you know it's not safe to stay.

Think about walking into a store, especially a woman's boutique, filled with beautiful things that you love to ogle. You walk in to browse, touch things, look at tags, dream a little. But as soon as you cross the threshold, you hear a squeaky, high-pitched voice yelling across the store at you. "Welcome to Such-and-Such! Can I help you find something?" You *can* say. "No, thank you. I'm fine," but more often than not, that won't do it. The saleswoman will circle closer, start making suggestions, tell you that the dress you are trying on, which is one size too small, looks amazing, when you know in your heart it doesn't, and pretty much make your experience miserable. I can't tell you how many stores I've gone into and turned right back around and left when I heard that squeaky voice come from someone who looked like they would be relentless.

Your memory is like an old vinyl record album. The thoughts that go through your head create a groove, and the groove grows deeper each time you have a similar thought. So for your whole life, you've been cataloging these distasteful sales situations and coming up with a conclusion that you would rather dig graves for a living than be that pushy, sleazy person in sales. Okay. That description might be a little drastic—the grave-digging thing—but I believe you know what I mean.

However, here's the funny—or not so funny—thing: These experiences are only one source of your sales blueprint. There are other things you have seen and heard throughout your life that keep adding to the blueprint.

Here are just a few more scenarios:

- Your parents may have made disparaging remarks about someone they knew who was in sales or experiences they had, feeling sorry for them that they had to take a job in sales because they didn't know how to do anything else.
- You may have sold Girl Scout cookies, fundraising candy bars, or wrapping paper, and remember your aunts, uncles, neighbors, and friends avoiding you because they knew what was coming. It made you feel awkward to ask, but you wanted to be a good sport, a team player.
- You may have watched movies like *Tommy Boy* or *Glengarry Glen Ross*, where David Spade and Alec Baldwin were portrayed as slimy, conniving sales managers and thought to yourself… Never! Never will I do that for a living!

Yes, all of these experiences, things you have heard and seen, things you have absorbed either knowingly or unknowingly, create thoughts in your mind about what it means to be in sales. And you don't like it.

And… it doesn't stop there!

When it comes down to it, your sales blueprint is built from experiences you have had and things you have seen and heard or been exposed to. From that perspective, it is built from the "outside in." But there is actually a second dimension to your blueprint and that is the part that is built from the 'inside out."

The outside in perspective is what I've been talking about in this chapter so far, the nasty experiences you've had when facing a buying decision yourself.

When I hear women say they don't like sales because they don't want to be sleazy and pushy, they are generally referring to what they have experienced themselves and what they found distasteful, and they are saying, "No, thank you! That's not me and I prefer not to do any of that stuff!"

Resetting that part of your sales blueprint isn't that hard. It takes a little work to change your perspective about what it's like to be a professional salesperson, shifting from your current perspective of it being aggressive, pushy, and self-centered to one that says it is possible to sell with integrity and mutual respect.

There is a bit of work that needs to be done to make this shift, but people can usually get there over time. We will talk about this more later in the book.

The bigger challenge in resetting your sales blueprint is the work you will do on the "inside out" part. This is the part that taps into your deep-seated, INTERNAL beliefs about yourself that are sitting just below the surface and can be very sensitive and tender—like a bruise you didn't know you had until you bump it. These are the beliefs that are formed over time that go way beyond what you DO for a living, these thoughts are the ones that create WHO you want to be seen as in this world and what you are here to accomplish.

When you are doing something that could result in perceived rejection or disconnection from others, it tests your beliefs about yourself and that is what stirs up your internal protector that wants to avoid discomfort.

That last paragraph was a mouthful, AND very important to where we are headed in this book, so let me break it down into why we have to focus on resetting your sales blueprint from an internal perspective in order for you to make the type of progress you see for your business.

IT'S AN INSIDE JOB...

The way I explain sales to my clients I say there is the "doing" and the "being" of selling.

To be successful in sales, you definitely need to know *what* to do and *how* to do it most effectively. That's table stakes—the bare minimum—and not very hard. You literally can Google "sales process" and come up with a million articles or books that would all give you advice on what it is you need to do to sell your products or services.

The real work, however, is in the "being" of selling—the internal perspective you hold about yourself and what it MEANS to not only sell to someone, but the perspective you have about owning your own business, being qualified to charge for what you do, and your thoughts about how others perceive you—all those things!

Simply put, your beliefs about who you are and how you see yourself have been forming in your mind for your whole life. Your identity has evolved based on what you like or don't like about yourself. The thought worms have been busy deepening these grooves over time and they are well worn and familiar tracks.

You may see yourself as someone who is kind and nurturing. Someone who is perhaps an introvert, quiet and reserved. You may be someone who deeply values integrity and honesty. Heck, I hope you see yourself as strong, smart, and confident.

Then one day you find yourself in a position you never thought you would be in. You are a salesperson, and worse than that, you have to go out and sell *yourself.* CRASH, BANG, BOOM…let the internal war begin!

Here's why, based on that "outside in" perspective of sales, you will be doing things that either clash with how you see yourself, or put at risk how people see you. There are no other activities in your business that ask you to do "hard" things more than sales. But again, it's not because they ARE hard. It's because, at a very deep level, they make you feel vulnerable or scared that your very identity is under attack.

If this is resonating with you, there is no wonder you have the perspective that sales isn't fun or something you want to "spend time with." In essence, your mind has been hardwired to see sales from a very clear (and distasteful) perspective AND at the same time, you are asking yourself to just suck it up and be okay with doing things that it sees as putting your identity at risk.

And you wonder why you procrastinate, avoid or just plain ignore those to-do list items that have anything remotely to do with selling?

Let's figure out how to solve this problem!

CHAPTER 3

FORMING A NEW FRIENDSHIP

So the question is how do you go from dreading or avoiding sales to having it become your new BFF? Well, it's like that old joke about how to eat an elephant—one bite at a time.

I do wish that I had a magic wand to wave over the head of you, the reader, and all of my clients. As I waved the wand I would say some silly incantation that would then eliminate all of your insecurities and fears and all of your misconceptions of what it really means to be in sales. If I could do that, I technically could end the book right here and we could go have a glass of wine together.

But alas, if it were that easy, all of us sales coaches would be out of work!

Forming new friendships takes time, just like the friendships that I forged with my Winey Women. We didn't become BFFs overnight—it started slow and then the momentum picked up, until before we knew it, we were the "ride or die" kind of friends.

When it comes to your relationship with sales, you have to remember that the thought worms have been at work for years, digging those grooves deeper and deeper with the thoughts you have about sales and the beliefs you have about yourself. Technically, in scientific terms, those grooves are called neural transmitters. I wanted to get technical here on purpose because scientists say that you definitely can rewire these pathways and change your thought patterns, but it doesn't happen overnight and it takes the same type of repetition that it took to create the "groove" in the first place.

But you are a smart lady, and I know you can do it, especially with my help.

The good news is that just like any problem you want to solve, the first step to fixing it is becoming aware that it IS a problem.

DIGGING UP THE OLD WOUNDS

For many years of my life I called myself the "ever-expanding contracting woman." No joke, I have gained and lost 50 pounds or more SEVERAL times. So to say that I'm a little sensitive about my physical appearance is an understatement. Adding to the weight issues, I am also well above-average in height.

When I was a teenager, I was always the biggest, heaviest girl in the class. And OF COURSE I chose to hang around with the teensy, weensy cheerleaders and baton twirlers—do people even do that anymore, twirl batons?

Looking back, I can see that I subconsciously compensated for not fitting in physically with my friends by becoming very gifted in the humor department. It was easy for me to find humor in any situation and make people laugh. I was eventually named class clown in my senior year while my best friend was crowned prom queen.

But secretly, I just wanted to fit in, to be the one who the boys looked at and asked to the Friday-night dances.

Believe me, I've done a lot of work on my self-image, but the old one still lurks slightly below the surface and rears its ugly head from time to time.

You may or may not be able to relate to my story about how my formative years created part of my identity—my body image and even how I see myself today. If you can't, I bet you have your own story. The one that lurks below the surface for you.

The reason that I know this is because throughout all my years of coaching, I haven't met one person who at the deepest part of their identity doesn't have a little piece of them that is wounded, that whispers—or even sometimes yells—that they are not "good enough," maybe even a fraud. And they're afraid someone is going to find out. Logically they know this is not true, yet they are paralyzed and shaken to the core when the fear rises up in them.

These old wounds present themselves in different ways. They're prone to appear loud and proud during high-stakes sales situations. Those situations when you are feeling most vulnerable and need to be strong and confident become a fertile bed for those fears to grow and come to the surface, just like when you were a kid.

Let's see how this plays out in a couple of common sales type situations you may find yourself in:

SITUATION: NETWORKING EVENT

You are walking into a networking event. You felt good about it when you registered, but now that it's time to actually go you feel dread in your heart and a pit of fear in your stomach. The thoughts going through your head sound something like this: This is going to be awkward; they don't know me; they all know each other; no one is interested in meeting me, and on and on and on, right? Fear of rejection is strong and comes from that old "I'm not as good as they are" kind of thinking. Even if it isn't real, in the moment, it feels that way!

SITUATION: MAKING AN OFFER ON
A SALES CONSULT

You are having a great sales conversation, really connecting with the person you are with, understanding their issues and communicating how you can help them. All is going well. And then it's time. The magic moment when you are ready to talk about your offer or give them a proposal. AND then there they are, those crazy thoughts again: What was I thinking; they are not going to want to pay THIS much for my program; they are going to think I'm being pushy and that I just want their money. Once again, this is a total story that you are making up in your head about what you THINK your prospect is thinking, but it changes the entire dynamic of your interaction and can sabotage your results in a big way.

Last example situation and this one needs a little bit of an explanation up front.

You may not know this about me, but I run two companies. My passion lies in Unstoppable Women in Business, my coaching practice. But I have also owned a sales research company for 10 years, where we study the behaviors of salespeople within large companies to help them identify what sales skills are connected to them bringing in the most revenue. We've studied over 15,000 sellers and have amassed quite a bit of quantitative data about what works and doesn't work in today's sales environment.

I tell you all of this for one reason only. The NUMBER ONE issue that comes up for the sellers from our studies—and is also the number one complaint that I hear from women entrepreneurs—-is that they can't generate enough sales conversations.

I have heard several women from the Success Collaborative say that if someone would just fill up their calendar with sales calls they would be as happy as a pig in a puddle.

Can you relate to this? Want to know why? Follow along...

SITUATION: ASKING FOR A MEETING

You've got someone on your mind. They would be a perfect fit, your ideal client. You can imagine how good it's going to be already, how happy they will be when you solve their problem with your solution. But this is all in your mind. They don't know it yet. Up to this point you've been "stalking" them. Following them on social media, maybe running across them in networking meetings, or inviting them to your Facebook Challenge. But it's time. You can sense it. You can almost see the dollars in your bank account. The only thing standing between you and them becoming your client is a sales conversation. But at the back of your mind, yes, there they are again, those nasty, little thoughts saying: Don't blow this one; this one is important; you don't have any other prospects this close; what if I am wrong and they really aren't interested? I'm not ready… I'm going to wait until I get better at these conversations.

This is a particularly juicy scenario because of its implications on our focus here. Underneath all these thoughts is a deep-seated belief in scarcity. Not only does the "I might not do this well enough" come up, but it is coupled with the belief that there aren't enough opportunities out there to sell to. And that is just a total lie!

RETRAIN YOUR BRAIN

By this point you are probably saying to yourself, "You are killing me, Susan! This book is making me so depressed." Hang in there, buttercup. We are headed into the fun part now. It's time to start talking about the solution.

If the problem is the fact that your relationship with sales, or your sales blueprint, was formed by some errant hardwiring in your brain based on past experiences and beliefs that you have, well, then, let's just change them!

Oh, but wait! You've tried that.

Right? I mean, nothing I've said so far is rocket science (I'm saving that for the next chapter). But I do hope that I'm putting into words what you have had swirling around in your head for a while and helping it make more sense to you. The truth is that most people know they have some illogical ways of thinking about certain things and have tried to "check themselves" when they notice it coming up.

But that obviously isn't enough... and because you are reading this book I believe you fall into this category.

As I mentioned before, your thought patterns have been deeply etched into your mind and it takes a bit of work to rewire them "permanently." Notice that I put permanently in quotation marks in the previous sentence. I did this on purpose because, technically, nothing is permanent about how your brain is wired.

The reason the efforts you have made to change your "mindset" have not really stuck in the past is because you have two very distinct operating systems in your brain, and they are at war with one another.

One part of the brain is logic based, but very slow to process. As you read and learn about managing your mind, the logical brain looks for the facts in and processes involved and works to put all the pieces together. BUT the other operating system is faster and more emotional based. This is the part of your brain that is always standing guard for you, looking for unsafe situations that it can hop on quickly using the data bank of experiences it has stored up and solutions you have used in the past. This part of your brain is lightning fast and will undermine any logic-based efforts you have read about, automatically defaulting to old habits if you aren't vigilant. This part of your brain is seriously thinking it is keeping you safe, when in fact it is keeping you stuck in your old way of thinking and holding you back from progressing in business and in your personal life.

So that's where we are headed. Let's dig into what it takes to begin the process of resetting your sales blueprint and overriding the emotional brain long enough to home in on what your logical brain is trying to tell you. And as a side benefit of doing this work, you will find that this process will help in areas of your life and business that don't have a darn thing to do with sales!

Rewiring your brain *is* a process and it happens gradually over time, but in a predictable manner. I believe it is helpful for you to understand the layers of change so it becomes easier for you to identify where you may be getting stuck and then to move yourself to the next layer and ultimately closer to becoming a sales ninja!

RESETTING YOUR SALES BLUEPRINT

As I mentioned earlier, the emotional part of your brain is quick to react and is standing at the ready to keep you safe. So a large part of resetting your sales blueprint is to slow things down, take a beat and then, at times, find a way you can respond rather than reacting to your "gut instincts."

Don't get me wrong. I'm a big fan of following your intuition. As a species, we would be nowhere without it. But your instincts or intuition can only be guided by healthy beliefs and a deep understanding of what is true and what are stories you have been making up for a long time.

So before blindly following your intuition, consider pausing and considering whether or not your intuition is leading you in a productive direction.

That's what resetting your sales blueprint is all about. A way to slow down and test the perspective you have had about any given situation.

To make sure we are all on the same page here, I define your sales blueprint as the culmination of what you think and feel about sales based on experiences you have had (external input) and your beliefs about how you see yourself and your identity (internal input).

Let's start at the beginning:

If this book is doing the job I hoped it would, you are fully immersed in the beginning of the journey to reset your sales blueprint right now! Your eyes are opening and you are getting a new awareness and understanding of where your blueprint came from and why it exists.

This may be a cringe-worthy comparison because I don't want you to think that I take recovering from addiction lightly, but I can't help myself in comparing this phase to the advice that Alcoholics Anonymous shares about overcoming addiction: The first step to solving a problem is admitting that you have one.

Because… you DO have a problem.

You need to realize that if you hold onto your current sales blueprint like a wubby, you will never be able to grow your business to the level that it deserves. It is that simple.

Did you know that 50 percent of small businesses go under within five years of their start? Most of them go under because they don't generate enough revenue to justify their existence. Your commitment to understanding this problem brings you one step FURTHER from becoming that statistic!

So many women that I coach come into working with me with a mild form of victim mentality. It's almost like they think their business is MAKING them do things they don't want to do, things that they aren't "good" at. No ma'am! You are in control of your destiny. You can do anything you want to do, be anything you want to be if you set your mind to it.

WATCHING YOUR BLUEPRINT IN ACTION

If you are a follower of any spiritual teacher, like of Eckhart Tolle or Deepak Chopra, you may have heard them talk about "becoming the watcher of your thoughts." That is the heart of this stage—separating yourself (the logical self) from the thoughts you are having (mostly emotional) about what it means to *be* and *do* the things that are required to generate revenue.

Some selling activities, especially the ones that you perceive as "hard," benefit from you taking a moment to examine what is going on in your mind, to step outside the situation and observe what is happening in your mind with complete neutrality. You can become very skilled at doing this because I'm going to teach you when and how to identify these moments and then guide you through a process that will help you codify it. I've got you covered for sure!

CHOOSING A DIFFERENT RESPONSE

At the heart of being successful in resetting your sales blueprint lies choice. Consciously choosing to think *and* respond differently once you become aware of the "thought errors" that your original blueprint was built on.

Oh, Grasshopper, Mr. Miyagi (the heart and soul of the *Karate Kid* movie series) would say to you right now, this is where the challenge lies. It is one thing to notice your thinking and how it is adversely affecting your results, but it's quite another to change it. This is why very few people can read about mindset change and make the leap to implementing it successfully. They need a step-by-step plan to lead them from where they are to where they want to be. And... again... I got you covered! By the end of this book you will have all you need to know about how to reset your sales blueprint by choosing to think and respond in a whole new way.

PRACTICE AND CREATE NEW NEURAL PATHWAYS (RETRAIN YOUR BRAIN)

Your brain is an amazing machine.

Jerzy Konorski, a famous neurophysiologist, was the first person to coin the term neuroplasticity in 1948. But even before that, scientists were realizing that the brain was always changing, especially in adulthood.

Here's the point that is important to understand. There is a choice that needs to be made: You can choose to live based on your default thinking based on experiences you've had in the past that formed how you have always seen yourself, your identity, and beliefs. OR you can choose to use these stages of awareness, curiosity, intentional thinking, and practice to create a new perspective about yourself, over time creating new neural pathways that will directly influence your success and, dare I say, happiness.

What do you think? Are you in?

If you knew, beyond a shadow of a doubt that spending some time inside your head, inspecting what's happening, working through a process to reset any thought errors would lead to better results and a more successful business, would you do it?

Well if you are giving me a resounding, "Hell, yeah!" Read on, Grasshopper, read on!

CHAPTER 4

STARTING TO MAKE THE SHIFT

As my parents have gotten older and are not as mobile as they once were, I've started enjoying taking road trips with them. For instance, a few years ago they wanted to go to Buffalo to visit close relatives who still live there. My parents live in Florida, and it would have been a hard trip for them to make on their own.

We talked about it and made plans that on their next trip to Raleigh to visit me (where they have finally agreed to fly to rather than drive, which is a whole different story), we would take the 11-hour road trip up to see the family with me as the driver, my dad as the copilot, and mom in the backseat cheering us on.

The day came for us to leave for the road trip and my dad asked me if I got the TripTik?

For those of you who are too young to remember, the AAA's (American Automobile Association) TripTik, just know that before we had cars that came with GPS navigation or even Google Maps on our phones, TripTiks were the best way to get from point A to point B successfully.

As a family, we NEVER went on a trip without them. It was Mom's job to go to the AAA to get them and make sure they were handy in the car. She would manage each page, marking off our progress. She and Dad lived and breathed by what the AAA told them to do, and it always worked out well.

But me, I don't even know if there was an AAA in Raleigh, let alone gotten a TripTik. I either used old-fashioned maps or now I just plug the address into Google Maps and off I go, blindly trusting that the one-step-at-a-time view of my trip will work out just fine.

I could tell that when I told Dad that I didn't buy into those old-time TripTiks anymore and that my phone app would be just fine, he looked a little skeptical.

"Okay, Susie," he said, "you're in charge."

But as my phone led me on a circuitous route of rural roads and small-town highways, I started to get the feeling that I might have made a mistake.

I had a sense that I wasn't taking the most efficient route, but I couldn't look at the app while I was driving to tell if I should try to override the route it had determined as the best one for me.

At one point, I believe that I stopped at a gas station to see if they even sold those old-fashioned regional maps. We bought one but were so far off the beaten path (superhighways), that we had to just keep on plugging along.

Long story short, we got there. It was frustrating, I had to put up with a lot of side eye from my parents, and it took a lot longer than it should have, but we got there. It could have been worse!

That story is a great metaphor for what happens when you try to reset your sales blueprint without the big picture in place without a map that will take you very clearly step by step and guide you through the process, so you can get to the result as efficiently and quickly as possible.

This chapter is going to introduce you to that process, and I think you will really enjoy it!

But first...

GOOD NEWS / BAD NEWS / GOOD NEWS

So in the last chapter, I shared with you the fact that it IS possible to rewire your brain and in the process reset your sales blueprint. Now we are going to dive into exactly how to do that.

Before we go there, I have some good news. Then, in full disclosure, there is a little bad news. But, finally, all good stories have a happy ending, so I will share the last tidbit of good news, the light at the end of the tunnel, the happy ending. Okay?

Good News: In this chapter, I will be introducing you to a process that will guide you through the process of resetting your sales blueprint. Just like the TripTik, there is comfort in knowing the full picture and how all the pieces come together.

Bad News: This process isn't a one-and-done kind of thing. Similar to learning how to speak a second language, you wouldn't expect to read a book that had all the words you needed to learn, put it aside, and say all set, I got this. No! Learning a new language, similar to resetting your sales blueprint, has to be done in phases, one step at a time. You start by seeking to understand and absorbing all of the things you need to know, then you practice… A LOT. Eventually, you become fluent and you can speak that new language without even thinking about what you are doing.

So the bottom line is that by learning and practicing the process I share with you in this book, you will be creating neuroplasticity and rewiring your brain. It does take time and a certain level of commitment. Are you up for the challenge?

Because....

Good News: It's worth it!! I mean, really, what's worse, feeling miserable every day, doubting your ability to drive revenue for your business and wondering if your business will stand the test of time in the end or doing a little work to get clear on how much of your drama around selling is just a big, fat story you've been telling yourself and creating a sales blueprint that will serve you for the rest of your life?

More Good News... everything you need to know is right inside this book. With a little help from me, you are on the verge at this very moment of creating your new sales blueprint.

THE STAR OF THE SHOW - THE MINDSET RESET PROCESS

All right, time to let the fun begin.

As we start exploring your mind, I'm going to introduce you to the star of the show, a solid process you will be using while doing the work to reset your sales blueprint. It is literally a TripTik through your mind.

Because here's the thing: if you ever started out on a really long drive, like I did with my parents, with just a vague sense of how you are going to get there, you know the feeling of being lost, unsure of what's happening and wondering whether or not you are making any progress toward your destination.

Well, that's what it's like to do mind management work without a process or a tool that will lead you along each step of the way. And that's where the Mindset Reset Process (MRP) will be invaluable as it guides you through your journey one step at a time.

The Mindset Reset Process will become your go-to framework as you slow down and watch your current sales blueprint in action and then choose a different response Then the same MRP framework will also become the foundation of your ongoing practice that you are creating, which is where you cement your new blueprint for life.

Here's one last thing that it is important to mention before we dive into what I refer to as the Mindset Reset Process. I didn't invent it. :)

There are countless thought leaders who have written books and published articles on how the conscious (logical) and unconscious (emotional) mind work together in harmony. I was first introduced to this mindset management process by my coaching mentor, Brooke Castillo, of The Life Coach School. I studied under her to understand the basic concepts and then the intricacies of how to apply this process to my life. I also have seen the same concepts introduced in the works of other thought leaders, like T. Harv Eker. Byron Katie and Dr. Joe Dispenze as well as cognitive behavior therapy specialists also subscribe to the same foundational teaching. They all know that if you can change the way you think about something, it will change how you feel. Your feelings or emotions will drive the actions that you take and ultimately the results that you create.

The process consists of five steps, and each step has an influence or impact on the next.

I can hear you now... "Five STEPS? Oh no!"

Do not feel overwhelmed. In this chapter we will take a look at the first two steps. I'll help you to get really clear on what happens and even do a quick activity so you have a chance to relate the step to your own sales situation. Then we will move on to the other three steps in Chapter 5.

So, if you are ready, let's get started.

STEP 1: GETTING CLEAR ON THE REAL SITUATION

The first step in the process starts with identifying a specific situation or circumstance that has been or is problematic for you when it comes to creating new clients. These are things that you do nearly every day and they can range from creating more awareness for your business right down to making offers to your prospective clients. If you think about it, making one sale can consist of hundreds of situations that you put yourself in or execute on and each one has the opportunity to move you closer to clients or further away.

Here are a few selling situations that come up frequently when I am working with my clients:

- Creating a lead magnet
- Adding new people to an email list
- Developing an email campaign to announce a new program
- Having a sales conversation/consultation
- Making an offer or giving a proposal
- Following up on an offer
- Overcoming an objection someone has about doing business with you
- Collecting payments from a client after they have agreed to buy

Those are just a few situations that you find yourself facing as you work to grow your client base. Notice that they are very straightforward and written without adding any additional emotion or flair.

At the time of the printing of this book, self-driving cars are just emerging in the market. However, there are still rules in place that, although the capabilities are there for the computer system to make all of the decisions necessary to navigate the car safely from point A to point B, a human still needs to be present and able to take over should the computer fail in its duties.

The reason that I bring up self-driving cars, or any robot for that matter, is that they are programmed with a set of very specific (if not complex) commands, a bunch of "if this, then that" statements. It's a black-and-white situation. Just the facts. If an object comes within X feet of the vehicle, apply pressure on the brake based on the speed of both objects.

There is nothing subjective in self-driving car capabilities. It can all be programmed into a formula that create a set of rules based on the facts at hand.

Let's apply this logic to situations we face in selling.

Because we have human brains in our heads (not computers), we see situations at hand, and instead of applying "just the facts," we look at the situation through a lens that includes both sides of our sales blueprint—the part that was programmed from the outside using experiences we have had and things we have seen and heard about being sold. Then we mix in the other half of the blueprint that comes from our identity and how we see ourselves when it comes to being the person who is doing the selling.

Once you apply your sales blueprint filter to any situation at hand, it now becomes less than factual. In essence, the thoughts you have about that situation create a story in your mind about what is actually happening. You begin to believe that story and a snowball effect starts, where a simple, pretty straightforward situation becomes a mountain you have to climb.

The key to the first step in resetting your sales blueprint is to get very specific in identifying the situations that have become problematic for you and isolating the facts about that situation—the facts and nothing but the facts.

Sales is one of the most emotionally charged areas that you manage in your business. As I mentioned earlier in the book, generating revenue (i.e., sales) can make or break its very existence. So it stands to reason that we can become very emotional about what it is we need to do to create clients.

The trick to the first step in this process is to look at any given sales situation BEFORE applying your current sales blueprint filter. Stick to the facts of the situation and get really clear on what the situation at hand truly is.

ACTIVITY: IDENTIFY A SPECIFIC AND PROBLEMATIC SALES SITUATION

The "buyer's journey" is a phrase that I like to use when thinking about each stage of advancing a relationship with someone. Most often you start as strangers, then they become aware of who you are and what you do, then eventually engage with you. You keep nurturing the relationship until you get to the point where you have earned the right to ask them to become a client.

Some people would refer to this as a sales process or a funnel, but I always encourage my clients to use customer-centric thinking, so I like to talk about it as the buyer's journey rather than your sales process.

I want to help you begin to apply what you are learning about the MRP (Mindset Reset Process) in this chapter. After a brief description of each step, there will be activities designed to guide you through a specific situation that will benefit from this work.

So begin your activity here and then we will follow this situation through the entire MRP.

1. List three things in the box below that you could do today to advance one step closer in creating a new client relationship.
2. Ask yourself these questions about the items in your list:

- Are the items purely factual, without any emotion or flair to them?

- Did you list something like this: "Follow up on offer I made to XYZ last Friday. Or did you list it like this: Find out why XYZ is avoiding me. Did you list something like this: Stop procrastinating on creating my email campaign. Or did you list it like this: Create email campaign. Notice whether you are listing facts or adding flair.

- Are these new tasks or have any of them been on your list and pushed ahead—day after day or perhaps week after week—even when you knew that completing the task would advance your revenue generating efforts? How long have they been on your list?

Reflection: Notice what it felt like to do this exercise. Most women I work with find it very interesting to strip away the drama from their sales situations and notice the unedited, unemotional facts of each step along the way. There is freedom in the aha moment that comes from getting very clear on the reality of your situations.

STEP 2: BECOME AWARE OF THE STORIES YOU TELL YOURSELF

I'd like you to think about the second step in the Mindset Reset Process as the story you tell yourself about any given situation. What we look to uncover in this step are all the juicy thoughts your brain is offering you about your sales situations.

What you will come to learn is that every situation is neutral... until you have a thought (or a bunch of thoughts) about it.

Let's take a common selling activity that's pretty cut and dry: creating a post on Facebook about an upcoming webinar that you are hosting. Let's say you created a nice graphic image, you've got the date and time, and you are ready to go out there and create a post on your business page.

Sounds simple, right? You sign into Facebook, up pops your feed, and immediately some posts from people you know catch your attention. So before getting started on your own post, you start scrolling and catching up on what others have been posting about. Before you know it, a story is building up in your mind about your very own post that you want to create:

- Darn, now I'm not sure this is going to work.
- My post doesn't look as fancy as so-and-so's post.
- I don't know why I am doing this; no one is going to read it anyway.
- Look at all of the comments on that post. I never get that type of engagement.
- I don't know what I'm doing, why do I even try?

See what's happening here? A very simple, straightforward situation of creating a Facebook post just turned into a full-blown story that has nothing to do with reality. The thoughts about the post come *through* the sales blueprint filter we carry in our minds. Although the post is a very neutral situation, in our mind's eye, we view it as a threat to our safety. The very act of putting something out into the universe for others to judge creates a barrage of thoughts designed to protect you from certain disaster.

Have you ever had a situation like this? I picked a Facebook post for this example because I don't know of anyone who hasn't suffered from needless stress based on the thoughts they are having as they scroll through their feed and compare themselves to others. Your primitive brain is on high alert and ready to provide you with an endless stream of thoughts to help reinforce the image you have of yourself... once again compliments of your sales blueprint. See how this all comes together? Amazing stuff!

ACTIVITY: DOCUMENT THE STORY YOU HAVE ABOUT YOUR SALES SITUATION

Go back to your list from the previous activity where you outlined three specific sales situations that seem to be problematic for you.

1. Pick one of the situations. Don't play small here; pick the one that can benefit you the most if you were to uncover the "story" you have about it.

   Sales Situation (remember, just the facts!): _____

   _____

   _____

   _____

   _____

   _____

2. Story/Thoughts you have about this situation; don't filter or hold back. Write all of the thoughts that pop into your head. Use a separate piece of paper if there isn't enough room here:

   _____

   _____

   _____

   _____

   _____

3. Review your thoughts and circle ANY that are factual, 100 percent true. These thoughts, if presented in a court of law, could be agreed upon by everyone who heard them.

_____

_____

_____

_____

_____

Reflection: How many of the thoughts that create your story are actual facts? If you are like most women I work with, I bet they are few and far between! Also, if you look closely at the thoughts that came up for you, you may see a theme or pattern that develops and shows up not only in the situation that you worked on in this activity, but in many other situations you are faced with in other sales situations.

It's important not to judge yourself here. What's happening in your mind is normal and proves you are a red-blooded, human being! That's why we do this work and you should be congratulating yourself for being willing to dig "under the covers" to understand and take action on resetting your blueprint.

CHAPTER 5

THE SECRET BEHIND THE SECRET

There aren't too many people who haven't heard of "The Secret," a book and movie that have been wildly successful since the early 2000s. At the very foundation of the book, written by Rhonda Byrne, is the notion that there is a three-step process for getting anything you want in life: ask, believe, and receive. Her theory that positive thinking and manifesting what you desire isn't new. There have been many thought leaders going back to the early 1900s who have espoused the same philosophies. When it comes to believing in manifestation, people usually fall in one camp or the other. They are firm believers, or they are active skeptics. I happen to fall in the middle.

I do believe that your thoughts have an amazing influence on what you can create or manifest in your life. But I also believe that you have to do more than believe to receive. First off, the belief part has to be genuine and unwavering. You can't just whisper a bunch of affirmations on a daily basis and think that things will miraculously show up on your doorstep. You need to have a deep conviction that has been built over time and is based on the thoughts you have been constantly thinking.

But there also has to be more than belief. To manifest all of the goodness that you deserve, your beliefs have to be followed up by inspired action. In my opinion, that's the true secret.

When you believe something to be true, for example, let's say you believe that you can help a lot of people and make a lot of money, that belief will have an influence on your state of being, how you show up on a day-to-day basis. Your state of being is the fertile soil from which all actions that you need to take will grow.

So the true secret is that believing in something with a passion can actually rewire your DNA. Changing the way you think can change the way you feel and your very state of being. And that leads us to the next step in our Mindset Reset Process.

STEP 3: TUNE INTO YOUR STATE OF BEING

Nothing makes me happier than seeing a booking come into my calendar for a coaching session with one of my Success Collaborative ladies. Last week I opened up my Zoom Office and in popped Sheila, someone I had been coaching for several months and always looked forward to working with. Some people would use the words "spitfire" to describe Sheila's energy. She was always positive and a true go-getter. But on this particular morning, I wouldn't have used any of those words to describe her current state of being. She was looking a little tired and I could not see any of the vibrant positivity that Sheila was known for.

"Hey lady! Tell me how you are doing today..." I said to open our conversation.

Sheila, in return asked me a question: "Have you ever woken up in the middle of the night, out of a dead sleep, to a feeling of dread?" She went on to explain, "I've been awake since three this morning. I couldn't stop thinking about the fact that I haven't signed a new client in three weeks and if I don't get going, I'm not going to have enough money to pay my bills next month, but I just don't know what to do next because everything I'm trying seems to be falling flat."

Okay. Well, now I knew where her current state of being was coming from.

What Sheila very quickly demonstrated in those opening moments of our coaching conversation was the very point of this step in the Mindset Reset Process.

The thoughts that Sheila had been offered by her primitive brain, in the middle of the night when it really likes to work the hardest for us, were thoughts that drove her into a state of fear and dread.

If you look back closely at the thoughts that Sheila described, there was only one of them that was fact: She had not signed a client in three weeks. Everything that came after that thought was a story she was creating in her mind. She was making up this story that she would not have the money to pay her bills, and there were deeper thoughts underneath that one. She saw herself never learning how to attract clients and losing her business in the long run. This story that was lurking below the surface is what drove the feeling of dread and fear and changed her entire state of being, how she showed up not only to her coaching session, but to how she was showing up all day as she went about doing (or not doing) the things that could create clients for her.

Sheila came into our coaching session thinking it was the fact that she hadn't signed a client in three weeks that was driving the feeling of dread and fear. She left knowing it was the story (all of the other thoughts) she was telling herself about that one fact that needed closer inspection. In order for her to shift back to her positive and go-getting state of being, she needed to rewrite the story she was telling herself about that situation.

Gone are the days, my friend, where you think that how you are feeling just comes out of nowhere. It's not true. And it is also not true that a situation is creating your feelings.

How you think, the stories you create about any situation are extraordinarily powerful. They change your state of being and if you aren't vigilant about noticing and adjusting, they can alter your potential for success.

ACTIVITY: REFLECT ON YOUR STATE OF BEING GENERATED BY YOUR STORY

Let's go back again to your problematic sales situation that you documented in the activity for Step 1 and then documented your story about it in Step 2. Answer the questions below from a perspective of what your feelings or state of being were when you were experiencing the actual situation. Close your eyes for a moment and think back to when the situation was actually happening.

1. Play back in your mind the thoughts that you were having at that time. What were the predominant feelings? Jot down a few sentences that name the emotion(s) you felt—was it frustration, fear, anger?

_____

_____

_____

_____

_____

2. As you replay the situation in your mind, recollect your thoughts and then name the feeling. Then consider where you were experiencing that feeling in your body. Was it a tightness in your chest, a cringing in your stomach? Were you feeling a constriction in your throat? Write down anything that you were physically feeling when you felt that emotion above.

_____

_____

_____

_____

_____

Reflection: Our mind is an amazing and powerful machine that drives so much of our lives, in the background, without us really realizing it. The bottom line is that the thoughts we have truly are subjective. We can decide what and how we want to think about situations and our choices will create our state of being. There is so much power in knowing this one simple fact: You are in complete control of your experiences if you learn to think on purpose. More about that in the next chapter!

STEP 4: NOTICING WHAT YOU SAY, DO, OR DON'T DO

Imagine this...

You wake up on Friday morning, pour a big, steamy cup of coffee, turn on your favorite news program, and settle in for a few minutes before starting your morning rituals.

Of course, because you are the consummate multitasking person, you have your cell phone in your hand and are scrolling through your emails at the same time. You notice that you hadn't yet received an email from that awesome lady you had a call with on Monday with her answer about when she will be ready to get started on the program you proposed.

The thought runs through your mind, "Bummer, getting ghosted again." You feel the frustration welling up. It takes a slow start, but you feel the tightness in your stomach as more thoughts crash in like waves on the ocean shore, "I really needed that deal to close this week. I really thought we were a good fit. I bet she thinks the program is too expensive. What do I do now?" As those thoughts roll through your head, the feeling of frustration turns into fear. Fear has a totally different texture to it. The fear tingles through your body and feels a little like small electrical shocks.

After dwelling on this uncomfortable situation for a couple of minutes, you hit the calendar app icon on your phone and look at the lineup you have for today. Hmmmm... Oh, yeah, you totally forgot that in an inspired moment earlier in the week, you blocked off two hours for making phone calls to invite a bunch of people to the webinar you will be holding next week.

What do you think the next thought that goes through your mind is going to be? Is it:

A. "Awesome! I can't wait to get rolling through my list and have some fun chats with all of the people who are a good fit for the webinar."

OR

B. "Crap! That's the last thing I feel like doing this morning. It's probably not a good time to be making calls anyway. I think I will post something on Facebook about the webinar instead."

End of scene.

I don't know about you, but that scene has happened to me, in various forms, on the regular! A somewhat benign situation—not getting an email from a client—gets built into a story line that is worthy of an Oscar nomination. So. Much. Drama. And it is all made up in our minds but has drastic consequences resulting in changing the trajectory of what we SAY, DO, and DON'T DO.

If you take only one thing away from this book, please know this: Procrastination doesn't just happen. Procrastination is one of the most damaging behaviors to anyone who is responsible for driving revenue for their business, and it is completely manufactured in your mind.

Let's just dissect a couple of things that occurred in the opening scene of this step.

There was a mention of how "during an inspired moment" you had slotted a two-hour block into the calendar for making phone calls. I'm sure you can relate to this, right? Maybe you had been listening to one of your favorite podcasts and the host was saying that the best way to create connected relationships is to reach out voice to voice instead of doing more emails or DMs. The host was also talking about their own phenomenal success and how they had filled a webinar and reached all of their sales goals using this technique. YEAH! You may have thought; this is the ticket! I'm doing it! Those thoughts drove a feeling of inspiration and you immediately booked time in your calendar to follow the lead of this amazing podcast host.

But by the time that task comes up in your calendar, you are in a totally different state of being. You may have had some nasty thoughts about someone who is "ghosting" you. Or you may be feeling tired or weary because you are thinking about how much you have been posting, emailing, stirring the pot, and not getting any responses from your people.

When you are giving yourself a mental beatdown, in essence believing the thoughts that your primitive brain is throwing your way, you find yourself feeling less than inspired and the procrastination lever is the first thing you are going to pull. The excuses will begin to flow. You and I both know that we can be VERY crafty in finding every excuse in the book to avoid doing something that we don't "feel" like doing.

So I have to really pump the brakes here one moment and state the obvious just one more time because this is such a huge point... FEELING inspired or conversely NOT FEELING like doing something (i.e., uninspired) does not come out of the blue, people! Those feelings come from low-level thoughts running through your mind and creating those specific states of being. Ultimately, what you say, do, or don't do is a result of how masterful you can become in noticing your default thinking and making a choice to either accept those thoughts and ride the wave toward the uninspired state of being, or decide to think differently and change the trajectory of your actions. You do have a choice!

ACTIVITY: WHAT DID YOU SAY, DO, OR NOT DO?

Let's go back again to the situation you have been working on throughout the Mindset Reset Process steps. Look back at the last section and recapture the moment, how you were feeling based on the thoughts you had about your situation. Are you there? Okay, then let's take a look at how it affected your actions.

1. Based on how you were feeling at that moment, what actions did you take? What did you say or do? List EVERYTHING you can think of. Did you do what you had planned? Did you react in a way that was useful? Did you spend time beating yourself up? Did you reach out to a friend and complain? Did you do some online shopping to avoid doing other things? I don't know your situation, so

it's hard for me to list all of the alternative actions. I just wanted to get the wheels turning for you. Make a list based on your state of being in that moment you defined in the last step.

_____

_____

_____

_____

_____

_____

_____

2. It is also important to ask yourself what you DIDN'T DO or SAY in this situation. Did you avoid doing something that would make you feel uncomfortable? Did you not say something that would have made a difference in the outcome, but you held back because of the way you were feeling? List all the things you didn't say or do based on your state of being in that moment.

_____

_____

_____

_____

_____

_____

_____

_____

REFLECTION: Are you taking a big sigh of relief at this point just knowing that there is a logical process you can follow to understand why you do what you do? Just knowing how this process plays out should be giving you hope for the future. As I mentioned earlier, awareness is always the first step in solving any problem. What you do and say—the actions you take or don't take—are the foundation of how you create your results. Knowing that you are in full control of your actions based on how you are thinking about any given situation should be comforting and inspiring to you.

STEP 5: CREATING PREDICTABLE SALES RESULTS

The number-one reason women come into the Success Collaborative is because they want to create more predictable sales results.

It's not that they are "crashing and burning" or that their business is on its last legs. They just have a sense that they could be doing better and have a deep desire to see consistent revenue growth, month after month.

When Samantha came into the group, she was on an emotional roller coaster.

Samantha had spent two years creating an amazing program to serve women that she knew needed her help. Her ideal client avatar closely resembled herself—a high-achieving woman who had burned out after reaching the pinnacle of her career. They were someone who had achieved everything they dreamed of but felt empty and lost. She had developed a program that helped them rediscover their purpose and reinvent themselves for the next phase of their lives. Her program was brilliant, her marketing perfection, her website and social media totally on-point. But her results... they were less than stellar.

Some months Samantha hit a home run and reached her sales goals by mid-month. Then the next month it was crickets. She couldn't convert a client to save her soul.

Samantha would express her frustration to me saying that she KNEW what to do, obviously, because sometimes it worked beautifully. And she knew she wasn't "going stupid" overnight. She didn't understand why she couldn't produce the same results month after month. What the heck was going on?

Through our work together, we discovered that Samantha didn't have a process or skill problem, what she had was a good, old-fashioned mindset reset issue.

Remember that I said when she came into the group she was an emotional wreck? Samantha wasn't sleeping well at night; she was frustrated most of the time. She spent a lot of her time (and I'm not kidding—a LOT of her time) beating herself up. Some of the regularly recurring thoughts she had about herself were things she would NEVER say about or to someone else.

The mental chaos was eroding her self-confidence and putting into question her identity as a strong, smart, and successful woman.

Is it any wonder that she was having inconsistent sales results? I mean, really, people! Why do we do these things to ourselves? Women are notorious for taking on the weight of the world and then blaming themselves for not being "good enough" to achieve the standards that we set.

Let's remember that we have 50 to 60 thousand thoughts per day and 60 percent of them are on repeat in our heads. When you are not aware or actively assessing what your mind is offering to you, those thoughts become deeply ingrained in your blueprint and soon become your reality. What Samantha needed more than anything else was a pattern interrupt, something that would help her become aware of what was happening in her mind and then resetting those thoughts so she could go back to executing the things that she knew would get her the results she wanted. The Mindset Reset Process was a life saver for her. As she looked at each step in the process, she saw clearly how her negative thoughts were creating a toxic state of being for her. What she was doing was not working because it was tainted by the feelings she was experiencing, the state of being she worked within on a daily basis wasn't conducive to producing her best work.

I used to work for a sales leader in corporate America that was all about activity, activity, activity. He would drive his sales team like we were a team of oxen. He didn't want to see us in the office. "Get out on the road and talk to people," he would say. "And don't come back without a sale," he would add with an unspoken threat behind his statements.

The team was terrified of him, because he also had a quick-trigger response to whether or not you should be employed by him if you weren't making your numbers.

So what do you think happened? People would stay out of the office, but not because they were having quality sales conversations with their best prospects. They would hide, avoid doing the things they really knew they needed to do. They were paralyzed with fear from the thought of getting fired. What was their result? They underperformed and eventually got fired.

So the bottom line is this: The final step in the Mindset Reset Process is where you can go to uncover how the actions you have been taking or not taking impact the predictability of your sales results.

ACTIVITY: THE RESULTS YOU'VE CREATED

Okay, one last time, let's revisit your problematic sales situation you've been working through and look at the results you were able to create based on how you were thinking, the state of being that created, and what you were then able to say, do, or not do, in essence the actions you were able to take.

To make it easier to do this activity, use the space below to outline the full five steps of the process for your example activity:

SITUATION: _____

_____

_____

_____

_____

_____

STORY you have been telling yourself: _____

_____

_____

_____

_____

_____

STATE OF BEING this story creates: _____

_____

_____

_____

_____

What you **SAY,** do, or don't do: _____

_____

_____

_____

_____

Impact on **SALES RESULTS:** _____

_____

_____

_____

_____

REFLECTION: So that's it. You've just learned how to work through the Mindset Reset Process. This newfound way of looking at where your sales results come from can be a game changer for you and the success of your business.

The intention of the activities was to help you apply what you were learning to one problematic situation. But imagine how many other situations you have faced since going into business and, in reality, over your entire lifetime where the outcome has been formed by each step within this process.

This, my friend, is how your current sales blueprint was formed. And now, by becoming aware and intentional, you can use this process to reset your sales blueprint for new and better outcomes.

WHAT'S ALL THE HYPE ABOUT?

Now you may be thinking, Susan, this sounds too easy, almost simple. Oh, Grasshopper. Do not be fooled. This simple little process can only be life changing if you understand the intricacies of how each step leads to the next and stay alert to when you are falling into thought patterns that won't yield the results you desire. I've been working with this process for over 10 years and still have times when I find myself, in hindsight, looking at the lack of results that I've created and knowing that if I had taken the time to reset my mindset, I would have achieved a different outcome.

But here is a fun little side benefit of becoming masterful at the Mindset Reset Process. While you will use this process to eventually reset your sales blueprint, it can impact so much more. Literally, this process can be used to help you manage any situation in your life where your current thoughts are not driving positive actions and you are not getting the results you want.

You can use this process to reset your thoughts about relationships, how you handle money, how you manage time, all the spots in your life where you are not satisfied with how things are going.

I'm not kidding you when I say that because of this process, my life has been changed.

So now that you have a good grasp of the process, let's work through how it can become part of your regular routine, just like brushing your teeth.

CHAPTER 6

PREDICTABLE RESULTS COME FROM INTENTIONAL THINKING

Before you started reading this book, I bet you didn't realize that you have been operating on a day-to-day basis at the mercy of your "default thinking." Now I'm going to add that this is how a majority of the people in the world operate, so don't start beating yourself up about this.

No one ever taught us that you have a choice in the way you think about things, that you can escape from your default thinking and decide what perspective you want to take in any situation you encounter. But now you know!

You have been awakened to the fact that if you become aware of your thinking, go through the process of watching it and uncovering the effects it has on your state of being and subsequent actions, you will become better equipped to create the results that you desire most.

Instead of thinking that your results are at the mercy of some outside force, you will begin to see very clearly that you have more control than you've ever imagined. Intentional thinking creates predictable results.

CREATING AN UNSTOPPABLE MINDSET RESET PRACTICE

As I mentioned earlier in the book, our inputs—the things we see, hear, and are exposed to every day—are what created that default thinking and the perspective we have on the topic of this book, which is sales.

The emotional part of our brain is always working to make us feel safe and happy. It also operates fast and is relentless in its pursuit of those things. But it is not always right. The primitive brain is not connected to your logical brain, so the thoughts that it offers to you are based solely on emotion and can lead you down the wrong path so easily if you just accept them as fact.

So your job now is to use the Mindset Reset Process that I shared with you in Chapters 4 and 5 to become an expert in living through intentional thinking. That is how you will eventually reset your sales blueprint and so much more!

I believe that every time you learn something new, the quicker you apply it, the easier it becomes to incorporate this knowledge and create new behaviors and habits. It's this repetition that eventually leads to resetting your blueprint with new, more effective thinking.

So let's get practical. How do you keep this whole Mindset Reset Process top of mind when you already have a plate overflowing with more things than you can manage?

I used this specific analogy because of the fact that I hear this from my clients all the time: "I'm so busy, I have so much to do, Susan" are some of the words they use to describe their over-flowing plates. They go on to tell me, "Yes, I understand that cleaning up my thinking will make an impact on the results I'm getting, but I'm moving too fast to 'become the watcher' of my thoughts, I just react to things as they happen and then regret it afterward."

Hmmm... Isn't that interesting?

When encountering these types of conversations and spending a few minutes in spirited conversation, parsing out what part of the situation is fact and what part is the story they are telling themselves, clients quickly find out that there is no such thing as an overflowing plate and that not much of what they have said to me is rooted in fact.

I just went through this process with a client last week. She came to our call in an overwhelmed state of being. When I looked at her through my Zoom lens, she didn't even look like herself. She was slumped in her chair and resembled a dog that had been kicked by its owner.

She opened our session with the words, "I'm not doing well. I feel overwhelmed and exhausted. I have so much to do and I don't know how to fit it all in."

I won't go into detail on the process that we used to uncover all of the things she "had to do," but let's say that within 15 minutes we had it all dumped out, put into buckets, and slotted everything into blocks in her calendar without any problem. The overwhelming amount of things that she "had to do" amounted to less than five hours of concentrated effort that she had plenty of time to fit into her calendar once she prioritized and organized everything that she had on her mind. AND there was time left over.

The way our brain works today is not that much different from when we used to think monsters were hiding under our beds as kids. The thoughts that stay in your head become larger than life and pretty scary. You become convinced that there is a huge problem that you are incapable of fixing. But when you shine the light under the bed (or in your brain), what you find is that the reality of the situation is far more manageable and there is nothing to be afraid of.

So here is the moral of the story. Quite often we create our own chaos simply by the way we think about what's going on in our lives, the situations we are facing.

If you are willing to dedicate time each day to intentionally practicing the Mindset Reset Process, after a short while you will find that this investment will pay dividends that are ten-fold.

Here is why I say that. Each time you sit down to work through the process on a specific situation you are facing, you will not only find a new pathway to better results for that specific situation, but you will also be building the muscle to make it easier and faster the next time you are working with the MRP.

After a bit of time, you will find it not only getting easier, but you will also find yourself becoming more proactive in applying the process in "real-time" situations. You will learn how to respond from your new perspective rather than reacting based on old thinking. So the time you have invested in being intentional and learning the process now pays off because you are applying it in real time and getting better results right away.

As you continue to adopt this new way of thinking, you are cementing the patterns in your brain and resetting your sales blueprint so that less effort has to be put into the process as it becomes an extension of how you think on purpose.

It's a little funny to me that nearly every woman who comes into my Success Collaborative joins because they think they need to know HOW to sell better. And yes, we do a lot of work on refining their skills and processes. But at the end of the day, we also spend a lot of our time together working through the Mindset Reset Process to uncover what is happening in their mind that holds them back from applying all of their new juicy skills.

I'm going to help you put together a very easy-to-follow, targeted practice. Then you can get started using this powerful process on your own, which of course is the point of this book!

Remember way back in Chapter 4 I mentioned that in this book I had good news and bad news for you. Well, to recap: The good news is that you now have the MRP, which is a repeatable process to help you achieve your goals and reset your sales blueprint. That's good, right?

We are entering into the "bad news" zone now. And relax, it's not that bad!

The bad news is that KNOWING the Mindset Reset Process will do nothing for you if you don't PRACTICE it on the regular!

I'm going to make a recommendation here that is going to be comforting for some and strike terror in the hearts of others.

Just like any other self-development effort that you have committed to— yoga, meditation, exercise, learning a new language, playing an instrument, etc.—to truly become masterful and receive the benefits of your newfound skills, you need to set aside time on a daily basis (or as close to that as possible) to practice.

I recommend that you start each and every day by finding a specific and regular time, grabbing a dedicated journal and a comfortable spot where you can spend 20 to 30 minutes uninterrupted, working on your Mindset Reset Process.

Have I lost you? I sure hope not! I've fully described for you the benefits of working on this whole notion of thinking on purpose and the impact it can have on your business success. I hope that I don't have to work too hard to convince you any further that spending 20 minutes a day to increase the odds that your business will not only remain viable, but you will be generating the revenue that you have always wanted makes perfect sense to you.

Hey! Why don't we agree to this: Give it a try. Commit to practicing the Mindset Reset Process for seven days in a row, then evaluate whether or not it is making a difference in the results you are getting from your sales efforts. I would be SHOCKED if you said that it wasn't, but why trust me? Give it a go and see how it works for you!

OKAY NOW, SO WHAT AM I ACTUALLY DOING?

If I haven't lost you at this point, you are probably wondering what you actually are DOING when you sit down with your journal for 20 minutes.

Here you go, your specific MRP practice outline step by step:

1. Out of the gate you want to PICK A SITUATION that you want to dive into. Select something that has been problematic in that you didn't get the results you hoped to achieve, anything that has been a fertile place for your brain to dwell and has been creating some drama in your mind. Below are a bunch of common scenarios that I talk my clients through and you will notice that some are directly connected to sales, while others are ancillary situations that ultimately drive sales in the end:

   - How you have been showing up on social media
   - How many likes or comments you have received on a recent post
   - Writing a blog post that has been on your to do list forever

- Creating any type of a lead magnet
- Creating an email campaign
- Building your email list
- Attending networking events
- Getting on other people's podcasts
- Calling potential clients to set up a consult
- The price of your programs or offerings
- Your website
- A sales conversation you had recently
- Money! How much you are making or spending
- And on, and on, and on...

2. Okay. Did you pick one? Write that topic/situation at the top of your journal page. Set a timer for five minutes and start writing every single thought that comes into your mind about your topic. Let the pen flow. Do not stop yourself, do not filter, just write, write, write. Fill the page with all the thoughts you have until the five minutes are up. Here is a pro tip: The juiciest thoughts will come after the three-minute mark.

3. Now I want you to go back through your list you just made of thoughts and circle the ones that are 100 percent factual. You are looking for the thoughts that are not emotionally based and that EVERYONE could agree is true. If we were doing this together, I bet I could wipe out all but a few of your thoughts and classify them as STORY. You are new to this process, so you may only get to about 50 percent. No harm, no foul, as you see for yourself in the next step. One of the benefits of going through this part of the exercise is that you will begin to notice just how many stories we tell ourselves about selling. This is a direct reflection of your long-standing sales blueprint at work.

4. It's time to pick just one of your thoughts that is NOT A FACT, a thought that is emotionally charged for you. The one that, if you were able to change your thinking in this area, would make an immediate difference in advancing your sales efforts forward.

5. Now the fun begins! It's time to work your way through the Mindset Reset Process using what you learned in Chapters 4 and 5 of this book. Do your best! Don't be afraid of making a mistake. This is one of the things you can do in life that, no matter how imperfect you are at it, you will still benefit from the process. And again, practice does improve your effectiveness, which is why I ask that you commit to at least seven days before giving up.

IMPORTANT NOTE: For people who like more structure than just blank journal pages, I have made room in the Appendix for you to do your MRP practice on those pages. Also, here is a link where you can download a copy of these pages and create your own customized journal/workbook. This is for my overachievers in life. I love you!

ADVANCED MRP WORK - START WITH THE END IN MIND

The structure of the practice that I outlined above will help you to create "muscle memory" in your brain around how to use the Mindset Reset Process for just about any situation you are facing. Just the act of dumping every thought out on paper will become cathartic and help you organize your thoughts and then determine which ones are useful (facts) and which ones are stories (drama!). Going through the Mindset Reset Process from top to bottom will then help you find opportunities to think differently to get different results on a regular basis.

But I think you are ready now for a more advanced approach to the Mindset Reset Process. This is an option for how to use this process in a PROACTIVE way, rather than waiting to use it when you are faced with problematic situations.

To set the stage on what I want to share with you here, I will reference the second habit **Stephen Covey** covers in one of his most popular books, *The 7 Habits of Highly Effective People,* which is to "begin with the end in mind."

I believe that another great use of the Mindset Reset Process is in helping you think through what the optimum approach would be for results that you know you want to create in the future. To do this, you would start with clearly identifying the results you want to create and work the process *backward* to find out what the ideal actions are that need to be taken, how you need to feel, or what state of being you need to be in to create them.

Mind blown? Wait! What? Susan, you diligently outlined a five-step process that will help me to reset my mindset and now you are telling me to go backward through this process? I don't understand.

Yes, Grasshopper, here is the magic of the MRP. You can jump into this process anywhere you like. It's not like double-Dutch jump rope where you have to be precise and hop in at just the right time. The MRP is very fluid. Once you have practiced it enough, you will find that you can work the process based on what you are noticing about the situation you are facing.

Are you sensing that your state of being is out of whack, similar to my clients who notice they are overwhelmed or feeling frustrated and avoiding doing the things they know will make the difference for them? At those times, you can start your process by describing how you are feeling and trace back what thoughts brought you there and what you are doing, saying, or not doing based on this state of being.

But what I am recommending for beginners who are using this process is to look at the results you want to create and work the process backward to find the best way for you to be feeling and thinking that will help you DO the next best thing to move you toward your results.

Here is why I believe this will be helpful to you. The most tangible and sometimes quantifiable part of the MRP is the last step—creating sales results, or lack thereof.

But whether you work the process from the top down or jump in where you are sensing there needs to be focus, it is up to you. Just know that it will become easier and easier for you to become really proficient at the five-step process the more your practice it.

THE TIPPING POINT IN RESETTING YOUR SALES BLUEPRINT

When people first begin to incorporate the Mindset Reset Process into their daily rituals, they begin to notice more regularly when they are feeling resistance to doing things that make them feel uncomfortable, like my friend Sheila who didn't feel like doing her outbound sales calls, or my other client who was feeling anxious about going to the networking conference.

An important shift happens—I like to call it the "tipping point," where the MRP begins to leach out beyond the daily practice time and embed itself as on-the-spot opportunities for an adjustment in thinking arise.

Becoming skilled in noticing your resistance and exploring what is going on in your thoughts that is creating a specific state of being in real time and being equipped to shift your perspective and change your outcomes on the spot —there's nothing better. It takes time to get to that level of proficiency in using this process, but that is what all the practice is about, right?

This is the secret, the key, the tipping point in truly becoming equipped to reset your sales blueprint. In doing this work, you will become a member of an elite club, a group of people who are "evolved" thinkers. They understand what was getting in their way, and it was always within themselves. You will be free to go and do anything without the irrational fears that have held you back in the past.

Creating an intentional mind management practice is something that you will get better and better at. I've been doing it for 10 years now and I'm not kidding you when I say, it has changed my life, not just my ability to grow my business, but my life as a whole.

CHAPTER 7

FINDING THE COURAGE TO CHANGE YOUR SALES BLUEPRINT

No good story can ever end with a mom telling her daughter, "Well, that's just the way it is, honey...."

I was about 10 years old and Michelle, who was two years older, had been my best friend since I was five. We did everything together, played house, played school—I was always the teacher—and we went to the playground to ride swings and play dodgeball.

Summer was always a magical time. The only rule Mom had was that we had to be home by the time the streetlights came on. If you are a millennial, I know what you are thinking. You may be shocked at the freedom a little girl had "way back when." But the time and place where I grew up (Buffalo, New York, in the 1960s) felt very safe and insulated from the rest of the world, and to be honest, I really miss those innocent times.

Michelle and I spent all of our free time together, just the two of us, in a rhythm that almost never got interrupted. Until it did.

Enter Kathy. The pretty, new girl who moved in a few doors down.

One sunny summer morning I woke up, gobbled down my Lucky Charms, put on my favorite pedal pushers and Paul McCartney t-shirt (we're talking Beatles here, this was before the Paul McCartney and Wings days), and went riding on over to Michelle's to play Barbie dolls, which is how we started out every day.

As I rode up to Michelle's house, I saw a pink banana bike that I didn't recognize lying on the ground just off the left side of the front porch steps.

I didn't think a lot of it until I started up the steps and, to my horror, saw Michelle and Kathy surrounded by all of our Barbie doll paraphernalia. A long time ago, Michelle and I had agreed to pool all of our Barbie doll stuff so we didn't have to go through the work of separating it out each day when we were finished. So on this day, to make matters worse, Kathy had MY BARBIE in her hands and was putting on the worst outfit in the heap. The one that I never would have subjected her to.

I stood there in awkward silence, not sure what to say or do. Michelle finally said, "Oh, hi there. What are you doing?"

WHAT??! What am I doing? What are YOU doing? Why is this person invading our space, touching our things? Why do you look like you are having FUN with her? You are MY friend!

That's what was going through my mind, but what came out of my mouth was, "Um... Nothing much. I was just thinking about riding over to the playground to ride the swings for a while."

And that's when it happened. My little heart broke for the first time in my life. Michelle said to me, in a smarmy way, "Oh, I'm going to stay here with Kathy." In my mind, I heard the subtle subtext of "That's so childish. Run off, little one, to your silly playground." She didn't say that, but in my mind, she might as well have.

I felt rejected and humiliated as I turned around, hopped on my bike, and rode back home. My person chose someone else, someone who was better than me, to hang out with. And that made me "not good enough."

I can't remember what I did after that, except my mom saw me on the porch looking a little lost and offered me a Popsicle to perk up my spirits. And so began my perspective about how food cures all that ails you.

But seriously, Michelle and my relationship was never quite the same. Kathy wasn't moving and Michelle seemed to prefer hanging out with her. There didn't seem to be room for me in that friendship.

I would see them riding past my house and hope that they would stop in and invite me to ride along, but they didn't.

And I didn't know how to navigate the situation. I wasn't brave enough to ask if I could join them. I was afraid to be rejected again.

It took a couple weeks before my mom noticed that Michelle and I weren't playing together like we always had. When she asked me what was going on, I told her about Kathy and how Michelle seemed to like her better than me. That's when she whipped out the "Well, that's the way it is sometimes" phrase and told me there were lots of other girls to be friends with, all I had to do was get out there and find them. Go on, go ride up to the playground and have fun.

My mom wasn't from an era where self-development gurus were chirping in her ear about how to help your young daughter navigate through childhood traumas. She did her best.

In essence, she was saying to me, "Suck it up, buttercup and move on."

I don't think my mom's advice is all that unusual. Think about it. When you face a situation that stops you in your tracks, causes some type of discomfort in you, the typical response is to either push it down, push it away, or cover it up (that's where using food as a distraction comes in).

In the case of my situation with Michelle and the "other friend," my reaction to being left out was to hop on my bike, pedal away, and then lurk in the shadows as I watched them do the things that I wanted to do with my friend.

And do you know what that taught me? Absolutely nothing productive. It taught me that when I perceived that I wasn't "good enough" to be part of something, the best thing to do was to crawl up into myself, think nasty thoughts, and feel bad. So what do you think happened next time I had to put myself out there to make friends? I think you know the end of the story. I never approached it from the same innocent place again. There was always this underlying thought that I could be rejected and found out as not being someone that they would want to be friends with, so why try?

I have a close friend who studies the "10-year-old self" and works with her clients to understand how experiences we faced during our formative years have trained our brain on how to respond in similar situations we face today.

The little girl who faced this situation some 50 years ago is still buried inside of me, so much so that I can recall the details of that situation in a vivid manner, right down to the pink banana bike and my Paul McCartney t-shirt!

This, my friends, is a clear example of how past life experiences create our perspective of what it means to be safe in the world and eventually impact our sales blueprint.

Within my story you can see where fear of rejection, fear of being ostracized from a community, fear of not being good enough, fear of losing my identity, of not being the "best friend" to anyone, created a story for me that it isn't safe to put yourself out there. No wonder my emotional brain is on high alert whenever I do something that risks any one of those things in the future.

It's a little ironic because if I knew then what I know now about mindset work, I would have taken the time to inspect what was happening in my mind to uncover what the facts were and what was the story that my emotional brain was producing to make me play small and stay inside of the house.

My brain was telling me that it wasn't safe to make new friends. That was a lie. But having that story run as a narrative in the back of my mind created a deep belief that I wasn't as good as someone else and that "no one" would ever want to be my friend.

This has been a belief that I have had to work on throughout my adult life. It has gotten in the way of my relationships, both professional and personal. And the sad thing is that it didn't have to.

I guess the moral of the story is that if you do the work to become aware of the stories that are being offered to you by your default thinking, they won't have time to get set deeply into your blueprint and you will be able to reset the thoughts, produce positive feelings, and create the results you desire because you are able to say and do the things that will come from that appropriate state of being.

The work that I am asking you to embark on can be scary because you may uncover beliefs that were formed many, many years ago and have been buried deep within a safe cocoon.

You may be questioning beliefs you have held that are no longer serving you, but the work to change them may feel uncomfortable and unsettling as you move through it. Please know that you can reach out and I would be happy to support your process. It is important work and sometimes you need a coach to support you as you move through it.

So now you've got your process and I've shared with you how to create a practice so that you become a ninja at applying the MRP and resetting your sales blueprint, but there is nothing like hearing about how this whole shebang has helped other sellers begin to make sales their BFF.

This chapter is dedicated to bringing all of this to life for you. I will share stories from the trenches, introduce you to women I have worked with (names have been changed to protect the innocent), and illustrate how resetting someone's sales blueprint has helped them to overcome the barriers that have been holding them back in growing their business.

The four women you will meet all had a deep passion to grow their businesses. They are courageous women because they all knew that they could bring in a lot more clients if they were willing to put themselves "out there" in new and different ways. Each of them had the vision and the desire to grow. In these stories we will look at what was holding them back and then how they used the reset process to find their path to success. Let's see if you recognize yourself in any of these vignettes!

This week I was meeting with a group of women who were going to a conference for a very popular women's networking group. They wanted to talk through what to expect, how they should prepare, and how to maximize the investment they've made on attending the event.

I was asking them how they were feeling about going to the conference and got varying responses from each of them.

Barbara said, "I'm so excited!"

I said, "Great, why?"

She responded, "Well, I've spent a lot of time getting to know these women over the last year or so by attending virtual meetings and I'm just really excited to meet them in person."

I asked again, "Why? What will be different about meeting them in person?"

This caused her to pause for a minute and I could see the wheels turning in her mind. She finally responded, "There are a few of the women whom I've met that I really want to get to know on a deeper level. I really think that if we could spend some time together, get into deeper conversation, we could find a way to collaborate or help each other."

Now we were getting somewhere. When it came down to it, going to the conference itself wasn't what was creating the feeling of excitement for this woman. It was the *thought* about deepening relationships and finding new ways to collaborate to grow her business that was driving the feeling of excitement.

To follow this thought process further, from a feeling of excitement about meeting these women and finding ways to collaborate, Barbara will definitely be able to take positive steps toward doing just that. She will be open and welcoming; she will be creative and curious. She is set up to achieve what she was hoping to accomplish by going to the conference.

But conversely, Sandy, another woman on the call, said she was feeling a little anxious about the event.

I went through the same process, asking her why she was feeling anxious.

What I heard from Sandy were thoughts about how walking into a room full of people was her worst nightmare. She knew there would be women there that she had been connecting with virtually, but she told me that her predominant thoughts were that they all knew each other and she was going to be "the stranger in the room."

Interesting. The thought of being the stranger in the room was what was driving the feeling of anxiousness. She thought she was feeling anxious about the conference, but how could that be? One woman was feeling excited about the very same conference that the other was feeling anxious about. SEE WHAT I MEAN?! Any given situation is totally neutral UNTIL you have a thought about it.

I can guarantee you that if Sandy, who is feeling anxious about being the "stranger in the room," doesn't change the way she is thinking about the networking conference, she might as well just stay home.

If Sandy doesn't work on her thinking, she WILL walk into the room with a closed-off, protective energy surrounding her in response to her feeling of anxiousness. This energy will drive very aloof, timid behaviors, which will ultimately not enable her to introduce herself with ease and strike up conversations that are friendly and welcoming. Sandy will end up leaving the conference none the better off.

Believe me, I have compassion for her. I bet some of you do as well. Walking into a room full of people that you don't know well can strike terror in the best of us. But knowing that it doesn't have to be that way should be comforting to you as well.

Knowing that the event itself isn't the problem, that it is your default thinking ABOUT the event that is driving your feelings, actions, and results should give you a sense of hope for the future.

What if Sandy was able to tune into the sense of feeling of anxiousness and paused for a moment to think through where it was coming from. Now that she is equipped with a thought process that will help her trace that feeling back to the source thought, is it possible she can see that she could choose an alternative way of thinking?

So that's the direction our coaching headed.

"Okay, Sandy," I said. "Now that you know feeling anxious is the state of being that will drive you to shrink back and not enter the room in an open and welcoming way, what would you need to be feeling to be able to network like a ninja?"

Sandy closed her eyes and thought for a moment. Finally, she said to me, "I want to feel confident, but more than that, I want to feel expectant."

"Ohhh, that's an interesting choice of word," I said. "Why did you choose the feeling of being expectant?"

Sandy said that when she pictured herself walking into the room feeling expectant, it created a very light and happy state of being. She imagined herself walking up to people and asking if they had met before online, asking questions about who they were, where they were from, what they did. She felt like she was going on a treasure hunt and was going to find the people she needed to meet in the room..

Wow. The work that Sandy was doing before going to the conference was going to change her experience completely. Once again, however, it isn't a one-and-done. Between the time of having our coaching conversation and the time that Sandy walked into that conference room, her brain would be shooting thoughts at her designed to keep her safe and playing small. Sandy had to keep adjusting her thinking to override the emotional brain and bring herself back to that expectant feeling by revisiting the thoughts she had during our coaching session.

Using the Mindset Reset Process is all about becoming aware of the default thinking that is causing the problem, finding a different, more intentional way of thinking that can be authentic, checking in to see if the negative feeling is settling down, and then sometimes repeating the process again and again until you get the results you are looking for!

MEET MARGUERITE—THE BUDDING COURSE CREATOR

Marguerite was, let's just say, an intense woman. She was a very talented graphic designer who had been freelancing for several years. When she came into the Success Collaborative, she had been doing okay with her business, but it wasn't to the level she had hoped it to be at. She told me she was stuck at one level of income for the last couple of years and couldn't seem to find enough work to break through that barrier.

I loved working with Marguerite. As we put her new growth strategy together, she was a willing participant, embraced the new ideas that came from the sessions, and seemed excited to implement her new plan with my support.

Marguerite had explained to me that one of the things that seemed to be holding her back was that there was a lot of confusion about what she could actually do for people. She found that people would come to her to do one small graphic design, like creating a logo. They didn't understand that a logo design was the outcome of a deep dive into how you wanted your brand to be represented visually. What would happen quite often is that she would need to do a lot of educating on what that process entailed. She would spend enormous amounts of time doing this over and over with each prospective client.

Some people would "get it" and they would move forward and do great work together. Others would push back and say they just wanted a logo.

Whenever I hear a client say that they spend a lot of time educating people and they do this over and over, I know that they have the underpinnings of a course in them.

I explained to Marguerite that offering a course is a great way to draw people in by expanding their knowledge of what you actually do.

Many times when I talk with my clients I use the phrase "curse of knowledge." I think that we, as business owners, know our business so well that we have a hard time describing what we do in a way that someone new to our work can understand. It seems that we have learned to get very creative in how we describe our processes and outcomes. This is most likely in an attempt to make it sound interesting or impressive, ultimately to differentiate ourselves from the competition. But what actually happens is that the uninformed consumer just gets confused. They don't really understand what we do, and as you know, a confused buyer will never buy!

Marguerite had a couple of different options. She could create a small course and offer it free as a lead magnet. Or she could create a course that she offered as her lowest level paid program. She could add group coaching to it and charge a bit more. There were so many ways that we could approach using a course to help expand the thinking of her potential clients and drive larger engagements for her.

You literally could see the wheels spinning in Marguerite's mind. She had an intense look on her face as she internalized the ideas that we had been tossing around.

After a couple of minutes of processing these ideas, I saw a shift come over her face. It literally looked like a cloud clearing away and the sun began to shine through.

"I can do this!" she said. "I love this idea and it could be the very thing that I've needed to do for a while. I can totally see how this would make a big difference in elevating the way people think about the services I provide. How do we start?"

We rolled up our sleeves and put together a step-by-step plan on how to get this project started. The first step was for Marguerite to create an outline for the course. I asked her to identify her key teaching points, organize them in a way that would flow well for her clients, and then come back to the next session and present it to me so we could make sure she was on the right track.

"Got it!" she said, and off she went to get started.

Fast-forward to our next session, I couldn't wait to see what kind of progress Marguerite had made on her outline.

Marguerite popped into my Zoom room and after a couple of minutes of catching up, I asked her how things were going.

Marguerite was looking a little sheepish, not her usual intense self.

"I haven't gotten anywhere, Susan and I'm really mad at myself. I was super excited about doing this course when we talked about it, but now... I'm just not sure. Every time I sat down to do the outline, all I could think about was that I had nothing to say, that no one needed to hear what I was going to put into this course."

Oh, yes, there it was. The emotional brain that wanted to keep Marguerite safe and happy was offering her thoughts and creating a story in her mind that she had "nothing to say." Based on what I have taught you so far, you should recognize that this happened because that emotional brain knew that Marguerite was about to put herself out there in a new and perhaps risky way, from its perspective.

At this point there were two directions I could take this session. The "easy" path would have been to remind her about our previous conversation. How she had agreed back then that the things she said over and over to educate people about building their visual brand was great material for a course. This reminder would be consumed by the logical brain and she would slap herself on the forehead and say, "Oh, yeah, I forgot!" NOT!!

Remember, the emotional brain will overrule and outrun the logical brain every time. So I took the second route, which was to start digging under the surface to find out what thoughts the emotional brain had been offering her while she tried to start on her course outline.

I spent a little time with Marguerite, asking her questions, digging around, being really curious about what was happening in her mind as she sat with that blank piece of paper. We did what I ask you all to do; I guided her through a brain dump all the thoughts she had about her course.

As Marguerite put herself back into those moments when she was trying to create the outline, she started to tell me all the thoughts coming up for her: What happens if I create the course and no one likes it? What if they take the course and say bad things about me? What if no one takes it at all?

I could have stopped there and coached her on those poisonous thoughts. But there was actually a deeper learning moment here.

When your brain offers you questions like it was offering Marguerite—what happens, what ifs—you have to answer them. If you don't, your emotional brain will answer them for you and the answers it provides won't be anything you like!

So that's exactly where we went next.

I said, "Marguerite, what if "no one" likes it (unlikely, but play along)? What if no one takes the course? What would that mean about you?"

Marguerite sat quietly for a moment. I started to see the beginning of tears well up in her eyes. She finally looked up and made eye contact with me. And she said, "It would mean that I'm really not that good at what I do and people will find out."

Now here is a woman who has been doing good work for many years and deep down in her heart she is questioning whether or not she is "good enough."

That's the power of the emotional brain in trying to protect you from stepping out and doing something new and different without knowing whether or not it will be successful.

Until Marguerite was able to reset her thinking and see herself as someone who offers enormous value to others, that course outline would remain blank.

The funny thing was that Marguerite had so much evidence of the value she provides. Once she was able to mentally revisit all of the times she'd had clients tell her how much they appreciated her work and how helpful it was to really understand visual branding, she was able to reframe her thinking and begin to feel confident and assured again. Once she was in that state, her pen began to fly and the ideas came and the outline was completed in just one sitting.

The course ended up being a huge hit and helped Marguerite attract more educated and qualified clients. But there was also a side benefit to this whole process. Marguerite became a devotee of the Mindset Reset Process because she experienced every step and it became real to her.

Whenever Marguerite senses she is stuck in creating something she knows she is fully equipped to do, she starts going through the MRP to uncover what is happening below the surface and find the thoughts that are creating problems for her. It takes a little work to find the new thoughts that will drive authentic, positive emotions, but it is well worth the time and effort. Doing this work becomes the foundation your success rides on. It's the internal work that creates the external results!

MEET LINDA—THE QUEEN OF PRICING DRAMA

At this point, I hope you are seeing how the Mindset Reset Process is an essential part of your business-building toolkit. As I have said, generating revenue for your business is not for the faint of heart. It takes courage to continuously find new ways to grow, and your sales mindset can be your best friend or your worst enemy in that regard.

Let's meet Linda and you will see how growing her business became a "mental" challenge for her!

Linda was an awesome weight loss coach whose claim to fame was in helping women lose their last 10 pounds and keep them off permanently.

Linda had been coaching for a couple of years and her practice was full. She had always been very careful not to not overload her schedule. She knew that she needed breathing room in between clients and also needed to save space in her calendar for "tending to her business." She was smart that way.

I work with a lot of new coaches who think they can coach from morning to night in order to reach their revenue goals. They soon find out that this approach is a recipe for disaster, but that's a story for another day.

Linda had a desire to make more money than she was currently bringing in. When we looked at her financial goals and started to put together her growth strategy, it soon became clear that to make more money, she had to do one of two things. She either had to raise her prices, or move into group coaching, or what about both?

I threw that suggestion out on the table to see what kind of response I would get from Linda.

"What do you think, would you consider raising your one-on-one package price AND start a group coaching program, Linda?"

We started playing around with the numbers, modeling what her new revenue streams could look like, and at the end of the exercise, we found that she could literally double her current revenue by making both of those changes.

I was watching her during this exercise. I saw her move through several emotions: excitement at the possibility of hitting new revenue goals, then I saw confusion in her eyes as she started to ask questions about how to do all the things necessary to move to this new business model. Finally, I saw fear creep into her eyes. I asked what was going through her mind. What I really wanted to know was what story she was being offered by her emotional brain.

Linda looked straight at me and said, "I can't raise my prices, and I'm really not sure a group program is a good idea."

"Oh," I said, "why not, what was just going through your mind?"

Linda started to tell me that she was thinking about her current clients. The fact that some of them could "barely afford" her at her current prices. As a matter of fact, she revealed that she had given several of her clients discounts on her packages because she felt sorry for them and thought that the only way to get them to say yes was to lower her prices. She also talked about the people on her waiting list and the fact that they knew what her current rates were and would feel like she was bamboozling them if she charged higher rates than they initially expected. Finally, she had this idea in her head that weight loss was very personal and that people only wanted to work with her one-on-one, so a group program would never work.

Nothing Linda said surprised me. It was a classic example of how, when faced with doing something perceived to be risky by your emotional brain, it will offer you all kinds of thoughts designed to have you slow down, rethink your strategy, and stay safe where you are by not making any changes.

The reason that her brain perceived her business changes as being risky is due to the story that was building in her mind that she may face rejection or loss of community. People may not want to work with her if she charges more or put them in a group setting.

The story that her brain was offering her was that her people already can't afford her prices and if she raised them, they would think bad things about her, possibly that she was greedy or mean.

Oh, the drama! Oscar-worthy scripting, wouldn't you say?

Without a coach to talk her off the ledge by using the Mindset Reset Process, Linda could have spun for WEEKS with all of these thoughts that her primitive brain was offering her. She may have gone another six months to a year before she finally decided to update her business model and her pricing.

I worked Linda through the same process that I used to help Marguerite separate the story from the facts when considering whether or not she could create a course for her clients.

Before diving into the MRP, I had Linda dump every thought she had about each situation (raising prices and creating a group program) on separate lists. We started with the first list—the price increase situation—where I had her take a look and identify which thoughts in her list were facts and which were stories.

We started with the thought that her potential clients could not afford her current prices. I asked her if that was really true. How many people have said the words, I cannot afford to coach with you? Wait! Let me ask this another way, what is your current closing rate?

NOTE: In case anyone is not familiar with the term "closing rate," this is a term that we use as sales coaches that helps us understand the quality of our client sales conversations. As an example, if someone has 10 sales conversations and three of them say yes and become clients (10 divided by three equals the closing rate) they are said to have approximately a 33 percent closing rate. That's not an unusual rate for a newer coach, by the way.

Linda said that she was running at a 60 percent closing rate. That means that six out of 10 people are saying yes to her during her sales calls.

Okay, let's run with that as the fact. Six out of 10 people say yes to Linda's offers. So it stands to reason that "no one can afford my coaching" is a story her brain is telling her, right? Let me answer that for you—hell yes.

Because I coach several health and wellness coaches, I know for a fact that there are people out there paying far more than Linda is charging— even at her new rates—for weight loss coaching. They are out there, Linda, you just need to find them and clearly articulate, with confidence, the value that they receive by working with you to lose weight and improve their health.

But here is where the MRP comes back into play.

As we looked at the thought "people can't afford my prices" and I asked her how that made her feel when she was offered that thought, she said it made her feel sad and discouraged. Even as she said it, I could see her shrinking in her seat, becoming small and tentative.

I asked Linda, "When you are feeling sad and discouraged, how equipped are you to publish new prices and communicate them to your clients and the folks on your waiting list?

Linda said she couldn't; that she would never be able to move forward with the plan feeling this way. I knew that if Linda didn't change her mindset about this, she would keep doing what she had been doing and lose the opportunity to literally double her revenue.

Just for the sake of time, I won't go deeply into the process we went through in looking at her mindset about group coaching, but you can only imagine. There was a story that needed to be inspected and cleaned up there as well.

In both situations, as we weeded out the stories and dug to uncover the facts, Linda was able to find a perspective that felt authentic to her and that generated a strong and confident state of being.

I wish I could say it was a one-and-done coaching conversation to put and keep Linda on track for achieving her financial goals. But it wasn't.

Remember, your emotional brain is ALWAYS standing at the ready to protect you from perceived harm. But, armed with her Mindset Reset Process, Linda was equipped to face down that primitive brain each time it raised its voice to shout out its warnings.

She was especially equipped to do this when I offered her an additional exercise to add to her daily Mindset Reset Practice.

This exercise helps to remind yourself of the truth and it cements your new state of being in a way that no other can.

I work with a coach and always will. Some people find that funny. They ask me, "Why does a coach need a coach?" Well, the fact of the matter is that you can't see your own blind spots. I needed to be talking with someone about my dreams and goals and the thoughts that my brain was offering me that was holding me back from making the progress I desired.

Remember, I'm the grown-up version of that little girl who felt like she wasn't good enough when she lost her best friend to someone else. The same girl who didn't fit in with the cheerleaders during high school. You don't think that my emotional brain doesn't throw the remnants of those situations up in my face on the regular?

One day I was talking with my coach about the fact that I wasn't making the progress I wanted to make in business and it was really affecting how I was showing up in my life. I could literally see my vision right at the end of my fingertips, but I didn't know how to reach it. I felt like there was a brick wall between me and my goal. This made me question whether or not—you are probably guessing it—I was good enough to accomplish my dream. I told her that maybe I was an impostor, that I was just putting on someone else's suit each morning and pretending to be a good coach and business owner.

And that is when my coach gave me the most valuable nugget ever. She said that in order for me to see my worthiness as a coach, I needed to do intentional work on my worthiness. She told me to start writing about why my program is amazing. She told me to write about it every day. She told me to be specific and write about how I deliver results and all of the little wins that happen for myself and my clients.

You learn to recognize your worthiness by doing this work, writing FROM a worthy state of being.

It did not happen overnight. At first it was hard to write about what was right in my life. It was hard to remind myself why I AM good enough. But if I didn't do it intentionally, on paper, my emotional brain would be offering me the alternative all day long.

Eventually, I started to notice that it became easier to notice and release the tired, old thoughts that came from my long-worn self-worthiness blueprint.

I shared this exercise with Linda. She is a good student. She did the work and became masterful at noticing poisonous thoughts entering her head space and was able to adjust her thinking before her state of being was negatively affected. It wasn't long after that she noticed that her pace toward her goal picked up significantly each time she reset her mindset and took action from a stronger state of being.

SUMMARY:

All the ladies in these vignettes learned valuable lessons as they applied the Mindset Reset Process to overcome some situations that became problematic based on how they were thinking about them. These are lessons they will be carrying with them throughout the rest of their tenure as a business owner and over time and with practice, they will not only become masterful at resetting their mindset about sales, but they will also be resetting their entire sales blueprint. Without sounding overly dramatic, I'm not sure how anyone can sustain success without doing this type of work. It would be like slaying dragons with one arm tied behind your back. Can it be done? Yes. Is it harder, will it take longer? Abso-freaking-lutely!!

CHAPTER 8

RUN YOUR BUSINESS
LIKE IT IS IBM

We are rounding the corner, baby girl!! Stick with me as I pull together this last concept that is important to your business growth.

At the very foundation of all the work that I do with my clients is this basic premise: There are two elements to creating a successful business and especially when it comes to generating revenue to sustain that business.

The first element is WHAT YOU DO—it is the culmination of your personal skill set and processes that you have in place to run your business. I believe that this element is table stakes, nonnegotiable. You have a responsibility to become very good at selling and have solid processes in place, a student of the art. With below-average sales skills and processes, you will achieve below-average results.

The second element of success, however, is WHO YOU ARE BECOMING—this is what the entire book to this point has been focused on. Creating a new YOU from the inside out so that when you get to the DOING part you can execute in the most effective way possible.

Big companies know this in a very acute way. They know that if either element is not up to par for their people, they won't make their sales goals, and that is not acceptable.

My corporate sales background was with a Fortune 100 public company. As a salesperson, our forecast (the deals we believed would close that quarter) was called our "commitment," and they weren't messing around.

Every quarter the company had to report to their investors whether or not the salesforce would achieve their forecast. So imagine this, we were just one segment of the business, but there were about 100 sales leaders who each had 10 salespeople they were responsible for. The sales leaders reported to regional VPs who treed up to divisional VPs. Each divisional VP would sit on a call with the president of the business segment and have to report whether or not their teams were going to meet their commitment to generate revenue. The stock price would literally rise or fall based on what these DVPs reported.

Do you think there was pressure that rolled downhill every single quarter on whether or not we were going to achieve our sales goals? Oh, you betcha there was pressure!

What the savvy sales leaders knew is that in order to drive success you can't wait until the quarter close is approaching to measure where you stood. They had learned to keep a very keen eye on how things were progressing so that there wouldn't be any surprises at the end of the quarter.

Now some of these sales leaders managed their team forecasts with an iron fist (like that sales leader I worked under for a bit), and some did it with a velvet hammer.

The hammer part of their leadership style let you know that the results you needed to create were nonnegotiable, but the velvet part came from the way that they would work with you and your mindset so you could achieve those results.

There was a difference in style and substance and it made a difference in the lives of everyone on the team, including the leader themselves.

WHERE YOUR ATTENTION GOES...

So why all this talk about what it takes for corporations to make their sales forecasts? What does that have to do with a woman entrepreneur?

A lot!

Tony Robbins coined a phrase, "Where your attention goes, energy flows." T. Harv Eker expanded on that quote by adding, "Where your attention goes, energy flows, and *results* show."

When a new doorway is open for you, like all of this stuff about how to reset your mindset for success, you may fall into a trap of over-assigning it responsibility for your results. I want to make sure you understand that managing your mindset is only half of the picture.

No doubt that mindset work will accelerate your success. I wouldn't have written this book if I didn't believe that statement. But it is also important for you, as the business owner, to have a very clear picture of the specific results that you want to achieve. And I'm not just talking about your top-line revenue goals. You also need to have a clear picture of how much activity at each stage of your pipeline will produce the results that you desire.

Remember: Where attention goes, energy flows, and results show!

I find that most entrepreneurs set a pie-in-the-sky revenue goal, stick it on the wall (if that), and hustle their butts off to make it happen. I don't often see a very clear roadmap outlined where they can measure elements of the overall goal and have it clearly show them whether or not they are on track.

Then they are surprised at the end of the year, when they look at the QuickBooks profit-and-loss report to find they have fallen short of their revenue goal. It's too late by then to do any course correction and they don't even have the data to look back at to determine what went wrong.

So as much as I am passionate about helping you make absolutely certain you are keeping your mindset clean and operating on quality thoughts all the time, I can't write a book about sales success and not include some sage advice about keeping your attention focused on the DOING part of the work as well.

And at the very heart of the matter, the two things—the DOING and the BEING—are intrinsically connected.

BOTH QUANTITY AND QUALITY INFLUENCE YOUR BUSINESS SUCCESS

Sometimes when you take a business related topic and correlate it with something personal in your life, it's easier to understand. Bear with me for a moment as I digress into my lifetime love/hate relationship with the scale to help me set context to the next important point of this book.

I have had a weight issue for as long as I can remember. I'm a good Italian girl who grew up in a family that had most happy moments centered around food.

As I reached my late teens, early 20s and became more conscientious about my weight, I tried EVERY fad diet that was out there. One that worked particularly well for me was the low-fat diet popular in the last millennium. (Wow! That makes me feel extremely old, referring to the "last millennium.")

When I got pregnant with my first child, the doctor warned me that if I used pregnancy as an excuse to eat anything I wanted, I would end up weighing 300 pounds and never be able to take it off. This stubborn, Italian girl loves a good challenge. My internal response to his comment was, "Oh really? Not me. I will show you how it's done, Doc."

This started me on a calorie-restrictive, low-fat diet that lasted over 10 years. I watched every gram of fat that I put in my mouth, and yes, I did lose weight. A lot of it.

I only gained one pound during my entire first pregnancy. My baby girl came out a healthy 8 pounds, 10 ounces, and I left the hospital weighing 19 pounds less than when I got pregnant. I managed to keep that weight off through restrictive eating and lots of exercise. I went on to a second pregnancy two years later and only gained 4 pounds during that time.

When all was said and done, I was down almost 50 pounds and was able to keep it off for several years by sticking to that severe, calorie-restrictive, low-fat diet.

All sounds good, right? Wrong!

While the scale was heading in the right direction, one indicator of success—my overall health—was not doing great. I became anemic, deficient in several important nutrients, and worst of all, I permanently damaged my metabolism, making it very difficult for me to maintain a healthy weight now that my hormones have gone on a permanent vacation.

What scientists have been able to help us understand now is that the low-fat diet craze that was all the rage for over 30 years was totally the wrong way to reach your optimum health. It ended up in creating long-term damage that far exceeded the short-term gains it provided.

Doctors and scientists now know that it is the QUALITY of calories that matter more than the QUANTITY in fueling your body in a way that creates overall health for you.

It still rocks me to the core that "calories in" does not necessarily equate to pounds lost. The notion that all calories are not created equal is something I'm still adjusting to. I have to remind myself on a daily basis that all fat is not created equal. Quality of calories is more important to my success in keeping at an optimum weight than the quantity of calories I consume. While I logically get all of these points, my brain still has a hard time when it comes to consuming fat.

Let's bring this back to the sales arena now. This is the same message that I want to leave you with regarding driving your optimum revenue.

The QUALITY of your sales *mindset* will help you drive the appropriate amount of activity (QUANTITY). With a good mindset, you will stop procrastinating and you will not hesitate to schedule and do the things that will make a difference for you.

But let's take that one step further. The QUALITY of your sales *activities* (which is driven by a healthy mindset) will have an exponential impact on the revenue that your drive (QUANTITY).

Whoo! You may need to go back and read those paragraphs just a couple of times to digest that little nugget! But here is the important thing to remember: These two things, quantity and quality, are intrinsically linked and you will never hit your true stride in business if you don't pay attention to both.

If you are out of balance on either side of the equation, you will have problems reaching your sales and revenue goals.

Too much low-quality activity will burn you out. Pushing yourself to do activities that are not well thought out and driven from a scarcity mindset won't create positive results for you.

Conversely, working on your mindset all day, but not generating enough activity won't help you reach your goals either. You will end up sitting around, thinking happy thoughts, but the proverbial cash register won't be ringing.

So it is this delicate balance that you need to be constantly aware of.

That's why I always encourage my Success Collaborative members to create a strong scorecard so they can measure the lagging indicators of their success, i.e., the health of their sales pipeline, stage by stage. And be prepared to course correct when they detect an issue at any particular stage.

Here is why I believe this to be the best approach.

When you are focusing on your sales results, it is the perfect opportunity to work your MRP backward! I mentioned earlier that the beauty of the Mindset Reset Process is that you can jump in at any step along the way and it still works.

Instead of describing this in an educational way, why don't I illustrate it using an example from my own business.

A HARD LESSON TO LEARN

A while back, I was doing my first launch for the Success Collaborative, my group coaching program. I had set my goal to have 20 women join the program during this launch and I set the price of the program at $5,000. At the time it felt right. I felt confident and excited about getting started.

Fast-forward to the end of the launch and what you will find actually happened was that I only had seven people join and I had dropped the price to $2,500 each.

So that was my result: Seven new clients, far less revenue than I had forecasted.

I was disappointed and a little discouraged because of all the work that I had done during the six-week launch period.

So I got out my notebook and started to work the Mindset Reset Process backward.

After documenting my sales results, the next step (going backward) was to identify what I did AND didn't do that led to those results.

I definitely *did* a lot of things. The amount of activity was there for most stages of the process, but... not all. I found that early on in the awareness stage of the pipeline, I ran a slew of Facebook ads that generated quite a bit of activity and signups for the webinar that I was running where I would be making my offer. So that was good.

I did run a strong email campaign, well thought out and well written, which kept my registrants engaged right up to the time that the webinar was being broadcast. The result of that was an above-average attendance at the live webinar. Awesome! All good so far.

But here is where the wheels fell off the proverbial wagon. One week before my webinar was going live, I went to a networking event and heard a speaker who was an expert at program launches. During her session something came up that blew my mind and eroded every bit of confidence that I had in my launch strategy.

This speaker was talking about statistics regarding the "right way" to offer high-ticket programs and it *wasn't* through a one-hour webinar, which is exactly what I was planning to do. She said you should never offer anything higher than a $500 offer through a one-hour webinar.

Whelp! There I was, one week away from my webinar and the confidence and excitement that I had experienced at the thought of having 200 likely candidates for my program in the room dissipated into thin air.

I started seriously second guessing my strategy. I was thinking, is it too late? Should I not make my offer? Should I change my strategy completely?

I was paralyzed by the feeling of being unsure. Not knowing if I should trust myself or trust this expert. Instead of taking the time to clean up my thinking and subsequently how I was feeling, I kept spinning back and forth to decide on what was the right thing to DO.

Now that you know the Mindset Reset Process, you may be skipping ahead and seeing how my "less than stellar results" had been influenced by the thoughts I had and the emotional turmoil they had created. Without cleaning up those two things, it didn't matter at that point what I DID, I didn't stand a chance of reaching my goal.

I went into the webinar, certain that I needed to drop my price in half, like that was going to help, and didn't feel confident that the audience in front of me would buy anything.

Obviously, I didn't completely crash and burn because I did pick up seven new clients that day. But guess what? These clients were the ones who would have bought anyway. Every single person who became a client that day I had spent quite a bit of time outside of the webinar with, nurturing the relationship. The people who didn't buy were the ones that came in from Facebook ads and I didn't show up strong enough to influence them into buying right away.

Luckily enough, I have been able to continue several of those relationships and they have subsequently bought in. But it was a tough lesson for this Jedi mindset girl to learn!

SPENDING YOUR TIME WISELY BASED ON THE RESULTS YOU WANT TO CREATE

Here's the moral of the story.

Your ultimate success will hinge on what you do every day and how well you are able to do it. It doesn't take a rocket scientist to make that statement. But what I want to make you abundantly clear on is the fact that you need to pay equal attention to BOTH the quantity and quality of what you are doing. And the Mindset Reset Process is your secret weapon to making this happen.

At first, you will be just like me with that launch that didn't produce to the level that I had hoped. You will find yourself in a flutter about something going on and you will react to the situation at hand rather than taking the time to sit down and think through the steps of the process.

Don't beat yourself up about this! Don't look back at situations that have happened and say, "Damn, I wish I had handled that differently." Like my grandma always used to say to me, "It doesn't help to cry over spilled milk, Susie." Weird saying, but I think you get my point.

Lean into the comfort of knowing that you are now equipped to create a mind management practice using the MRP to guide your intentional thinking and ultimately the results you will be creating. Somewhere down the line, you will become more proficient at catching yourself IN THE MOMENT and become equipped to course correct much faster and more easily. Your new blueprint will begin to form and get stronger every day.

I have faith in you! Once you experience the process, your life will never be the same.

CHAPTER 9

LET'S PUT A BOW ON THIS

Gosh, I sure hope this book has been helpful for you. If you are reading this last little chapter, I'm guessing that I was able to hold your attention AND provide information that will be useful to your future success.

Let's just sum it all up here and put a tidy little bow on it.

MAKING SALES YOUR NEW BFF WILL TAKE A FEW THINGS.....

Let's start here: Please make peace with the fact that if you own a business, you ARE in sales, and that it is not a horrible thing.

Saying things like: I don't like sales, it makes me feel pushy or sleazy, will lead you to doing things that will make you feel, you guessed it, sleazy or pushy!

Be proud of the fact that you and your business provide amazing value to the right customer. Make certain that you enter into any sales activity with a mindset of being proud of what you do and how you help people.

xt, the more you work to understand where your sales blueprint came from and focus on resetting the parts that don't serve you, the faster you will find that sales can be fun! Remember that your sales blueprint is a combination of both your external experiences in life—what you have seen and heard from others—and the internal perspective you have on your own self-worth.

Another key to your success lies in how closely you pay attention to your sales mindset on a day-to-day basis. Notice when you are feeling off and don't ignore the subtle indicators that are telling you to spend a little time with your journal and the Mindset Reset Process.

Setting aside time to intentionally and regularly practice thinking on purpose will be the key to rewiring your brain to think thoughts that are useful and will yield quality results for your business.

The reset process will never be complete; it is a work in progress and can be a wonderful journey as you watch yourself evolve into an amazing businesswoman. Mark this date on the calendar. Then go and do your mindset work on a regular basis. I can promise you that one year from now you won't even recognize who you have become.

I can't wait to watch it happen! Let me know how you are finding this work and the difference it is making in your sales results. I do care. Keep in touch!!

Your new sales BFF,
Susan

APPENDIX

As I stressed several times throughout this book, your success in making sales your new BFF will depend on how much quality time you spend thinking about her and exploring that relationship.

One of my recommendations is to create a mindset reset practice where you journal on a daily basis in a very specific way. This process is outlined in Chapter 6.

This appendix is an expanded example of the format that I shared with you in that chapter and can serve to get you started creating your own journal.

Seriously, your journal can be just a blank notebook that gives you the freedom to run through the process on a daily basis. But my clients tell me that having the structure of these pages does help keep them on track.

Try it! Use these pages and see how it feels. If you like it, feel free to go to my book resources and download the pdf version of this appendix so that you can print multiple copies and create a notebook that keeps all of your journaling in one place.

No matter which method you choose, the important thing is that you commit to the practice so that you can literally watch your sales blueprint change.

Good luck!! Let me know how I can help.

UNSTOPPABLE MINDSET RESET RESOURCES PAGE LINK

Download the PDF now by scanning the QR code below.